EXCLUSIVE BONUSES FOR YOUR SHADOW WORK JOURNEY

Welcome to the bonus page of my shadow work book! I have prepared two special gifts for you that you can obtain by downloading the files through the QR code below.

BONUS #1: 21-DAY SHADOW PLAN

That I want to share with you is a special 21-day set of tools for shadow work. This set will provide you with all the necessary tools and exercises to create a personalized shadow work plan to implement in your daily life.

BONUS #2: 5 DEEP EXERCISES TO EXPLORE YOUR SHADOW AND UNDERSTAND YOUR ARCHETYPES

The second bonus that I offer is a series of guided and additional exercises to the books on shadow work. These exercises will help you deepen your work on the shadow and further develop your self-awareness.

I am excited to offer these bonuses to my readers and hope that they will help you further progress in your shadow work journey. Do not hesitate to download the files through the QR code below to access the bonuses and start exploring your shadow right away!

THE SHADOW WORK WORKBOOK

A Transformative Self-Care Journey to Heal Past Traumas, Awaken Your Inner Child, and Uncover Your Authentic Self with Empowering Exercises & Prompts

Scarlett Kent

About this Shadow Workbook

Before reading this book, read this short section to know if this Shadow Workbook is for you or not. The purpose of this Workbook is to help you self-analyze so that you can eliminate your anxiety and negativity. To do this, the Shadow Workbook will follow a clear and concise path for your 21 Day journey. This 21 Day journey is your path to getting to know your inner child and your authentic self.

While you embark on your journey of self-actuation and get to know your inner child, there will be daily exercises for you to do. Each day you complete these exercises, you will check off a day on your Shadow Plan calendar. Every exercise that you do every day will help you explore your four main archetypes. These archetypes are the different parts of yourself that reside in your unconscious mind. Carl Jung said that it is the unconscious mind that dictates our daily life as well as the world around us.

As Carl Jung said, you need to keep in mind the world that is around you during your Shadow Plan journey. Your surroundings or environment can play a role in how you see yourself and, in turn, cause anxiety or negativity. While you're using this Shadow Workbook, you will be asked to observe your daily life and how you feel about the way people treat you. Along with this, it's important to evaluate the way that you treat yourself or look at yourself. It's important to follow the path of this workbook and stay dedicated to self-improvement for all 21 days.

TABLE OF CONTENTS

THE BENEFITS OF SHADOW WORK

Transform your life

Overcome fears & traumas

Love yourself

Light up your shadow

Self-acceptance

Become 100% authentic

Deep self-awareness

THE WORKBOOK PATH

The path of this Workbook is specially designed to help you get to know your inner and authentic child and self through the exercises. These exercises are given to you as a tool to put the information that you'll learn to practical use and help you apply it. The information or content in this Workbook is Carl Jung's own works and his approach to psychology, explaining that our inner child dictates our own lives. He even devised methods to extract information about your inner child from your unconscious mind.

The content in this Workbook to help you extract this information is meditation techniques. The things that you would meditate on or contemplate are your four main archetypes and possible repressed ideas. You will learn about these repressed ideas and feelings while observing physical reactions to others or different thoughts. The exercises listed in this Workbook will help you learn about those repressed ideas and feelings.

Two exercises in this Workbook are a letter to your future self and a trigger log. The letter to your future self-extracts information about your desires and your hopes about where you wish to be. One of the reasons for this exercise is to also hope you imagine your life without anxiety and negativity. When you do, you'll begin to desire that life more and more, which invokes motivation for change. On the other hand, the trigger log exercise helps you identify the problems in your life. Sometimes we don't have the motivation to speak up when we feel wrong, and our body instinctually reacts. The build-up of these reactions to the negativity in our life causes anxiety and negativity. You will be expected to either make changes, so these reactions don't occur or instead complete a gratitude exercise to recharge your emotional batteries. It is the balance within yourself and acknowledging the authentic self that will give you relief from your anxiety or negativity.

To get to know your authentic self and create balance within yourself, it's important to get to know your four main archetypes. The content within this Workbook will go into great detail about this. You will also learn techniques to dive into your unconscious mind, which is what enables you to learn about your four main archetypes.

The exercises and techniques afforded to you in this Workbook will help you explore your desires and repressed feelings. You will take a trip through an exploration of your unconscious mind.

Exploring your unconscious mind may seem like a hard task, and you may get discouraged. If you do, remember that Carl Jung's methods of using the four main archetypes have helped many people live a better and more fulfilling life. If you have a broken bone or ear infection, you will go to a doctor, because they specialize in that area of expertise. In regard to how the mind works and the ways it can be modified, Carl Jung is a specialist in this area of expertise. It only makes sense that you would want advice from someone who has a vast knowledge of the topic that you are exploring.

You have made a good decision in choosing to learn about Carl Jung's four main archetypes. His methods will enable you to explore these four main archetypes in the comfort of your everyday life. With the methods listed in this Shadow Workbook, you will be able to begin your journey into your unconscious mind.

Why Use Carl Jung's Four Main Archetypes?

This journey into your unconscious mind will be into your Shadow, Persona, Anima, and Self. Exploring your desires, repressed ideas, and how the world sees you will afford you the knowledge of why you have anxiety and negativity. It's the exploration of these four main archetypes that will help you get to know your authentic self. We all have things about ourselves that we don't like, and during your journey, you will be able to get to the source of those things. Only through knowing yourself better can you begin to accept these characteristics about yourself. Once you accept them all, you can live a fuller life without anxiety and negativity.

If the source of your anxiety and negativity was in your everyday life and your conscious mind, you would need this Workbook. It will be with the use of Carl Jung's four main archetypes that you will be able to eliminate your anxiety and negativity. It's not uncommon for the four main archetypes to be affecting your daily life negatively enough. There is a lot in the world today to distract us and make it not a priority to change so that we are happier. Instant happiness can be found in watching our favorite shows and listening to the music that we like with a few easy taps on our phones. This instant happiness will last but a short time, which is why using this Shadow Workbook will help you in the long term.

You Could Use This Workbook If...

Social anxiety and negative thoughts about yourself can be helped by using Carl Jung's methods. If you feel like you're not living your full life, it's possibly because you have desires that are not being recognized and fulfilled. This book can be used to help you fulfill those very desires that are residing in your unconscious mind. You're reading this Workbook because you want to improve yourself and your life, so let's do it. Start using it and eliminate your anxiety and negativity.

If, after reading this, you choose to continue to read and use this book, it's time to start dedicating yourself to it. On the next page is this Workbook belongs-to declaration. You'll need to decide to dedicate yourself fully to this journey of getting to know yourself better. It's important to keep an open mind, so put your inhibitions aside and fill in that page.

"To confront a person with his shadow is to show him his own light."

- Carl Jung -

USING THIS WORKBOOK

When you begin using this Workbook, you may feel anxious about a lot of things. For example, you may feel anxious about being in a large group of people. In the beginning, before using this Workbook, you may even find it difficult to talk to people at work and make friends. While some days may seem hard, there is hope at the end of the tunnel awaiting you after your hard work. You can move past these feelings and eliminate your negativity and anxiety. If you begin using this Workbook to extinguish your negativity and or anxiety, you must be determined to see it through.

Do Nothing and Get Worse

By not working throw your anxiety and/or negativity, you will be allowing it to get worse. They will begin to bottle up like a shaken pop bottle. After a while, you will explode and no longer be able to function. It is essential that you take up your Workbook and begin your journey of self-improvement. You will begin your exploration of your inner child so that you can be your best self. By using this book with clear intentions and determination, you can get tangible, realistic results.

Workbook Results

If you want results and to improve yourself, then use this Workbook to the fullest. You don't have to be anxious when talking to coworkers. Being in a large group of people doesn't have to make you anxious but can bring you joy and make you happy. After using this book, you could dress the way you want and say what you want with full confidence in yourself. Say it loud and proud! You are strong, and you can do this.

PREFACE

Live not just to live, but to feel alive and self-aware. By asking yourself the question "why then dig deep into our inner child?", you can open a fascinating door. Why do some start the day off with a coffee and others with a cup of green tea? Could there be a reason why some get dressed first thing in the morning, as opposed to waiting till they walk out the door? The use of Shadow Workbook can be used by all as a tool to analyze their inner child by implementing Carl Jung's methods. These same methods can answer questions like "Why do I procrastinate?" and can also be applied to help remove anxiety and negativity just as effectively.

Hypothetically speaking, for example, you may be anxious about going about in public or entering a face-to-face social situation. It could be that you have very negative thoughts about your body or a particular physical characteristic. If either of these would apply to you, Carl Jung's methods and this Shadow Workbook could be just the tool you need to explore these real, understandable anxieties or negative thoughts. If so, then this book is for you, and the exercises in the daily explorations could very well help you.

One of the experiences that lie within this Shadow Workbook is a daily reminder to tell yourself that you are beautiful just the way you are and that whatever your particular characteristic or characteristics that you find undesirable are what make you unique. Your particular uniqueness is to be cherished and valued because it is priceless. This particular daily exercise is to tell yourself, "I love all my unique body characteristics, and I am worth being cherished because I am invaluable," in a mirror every morning while you brush your teeth or wash your face. You could use this exercise, and many more like it, to alleviate those anxious or negative thoughts that you are experiencing.

Carl Jung proposed with the Self archetype that anyone could see their self-worth and, with this knowledge, overcome any negative thoughts and/or anxiety.

The Persona archetype can help us understand why we feel like we aren't accepted by our peers. If our Persona archetype is in stark contrast or in conflict with our Self archetype, feelings of alienation can form in both our conscious and subconscious. It's possible for the characteristics that lie within our Shadow or Anima archetypes to be the source. It is these conflict warning within us that often cause anxiety and negativity. Carl Jung's methods within the exercises in this Shadow Workbook can help you explore this authentic self within your subconscious to ultimately relieve your anxieties and negativity.

INTRODUCTION

Have you ever thought that your behaviors are like those of your parents or grandparents? It is well established that children often walk or even talk the way their parents do. Carl Jung proposed that we inherit archetypes much like these inherited behaviors and proposed that there are four major archetypes. The four major archetypes are as listed: the Shadow, the Persona, the Anima / Animus, and the Self. Although, because they are inherited at such a young age, we must look to our subconscious or inner child to endeavor to root out the origin and its effect on our daily lives. This Shadow Workbook tries to explore the subconscious and bring these archetypes to the surface for analysis.

One of the archetypes that Jung proposed has been called the Shadow, which, as stated before, lies within the unconscious mind. It is made up of repressed ideas, wishes, impulses, and shortcomings. This Shadow contains the attributes of ourselves that we recognize are unacceptable to society and our own morals or beliefs. Carl Jung proposed that to fully know oneself, it is necessary to recognize and explore our Shadow archetype. This shadow can come forward and appear in dreams or visions in both a literal sense and through symbolism, and by analyzing this, one may attempt to analyze their shadow.

Another archetype this book endeavors to analyze is the Animus or Anima, which is the feminine appearance found within a male or the masculine appearance found within a female. Carl Jung postulated that these appearances contribute to our gender identity and even sexual roles. Considering society's rigid gender roles, an Anima would pose defiance to social norms and would be pushed to the subconscious. By looking in the mirror and participating in this Shadow Workbook exercises, it becomes possible to analyze this particular archetype, as well as the others, using the exercises in this Shadow Workbook.

Looking in the mirror, the Persona archetype can also begin to surface through the exercises in the Shadow Workbook. One's Persona is a mask or change in behavior that can be contributed to a certain social setting or persons in attendance. Carl Jung postulates that this persona or mask develops to shield us and suppress our urges. In direct correlation with emotional outbursts, not being socially acceptable in a public environment will create a persona to suppress the impulse. While one's Persona could arguably be a characteristic of oneself, Carl Jung would say that the Self is another thing altogether.

The archetype of the Self is comprised of both the unconscious and subconscious within a person. Within your unconscious and subconscious, there are personality traits that exist, which in turn are the Self. Every attribute and characteristic that lie within and make up someone's personality, knowing or unknowing, can be attributed to the Self archetype. As Carl Jung often explained, it is like a circle with a dot in the center, representing one's ego, and the circle being the Self. The relationship between your ego and the Self archetype is what gives it its importance. The Shadow Workbook daily entries will guide you on a path and help you analyze each one of these archetypes within yourself. Through self-awareness and understanding comes growth and personal knowledge. After finishing and participating in each daily exercise, it is hoped that you can find a deeper understanding of your inner child.While your inner child or unconscious is not obviously there, it is undoubtedly prevalent in your daily life. The unconscious mind is a powerful force with our personality / inner child that ultimately dictates our actions or reactions.

Carl Jung would say that the unconscious mind rules our lives and that only by understanding our unconscious mind and inner child we truly take hold of our lives. Take back your power, explore your unconscious mind, and get to know your inner child. It will no longer rule your day and cause you anxiety or negativity because you're taking back the power. Ultimately, this is how you can self-improve and get rid of your anxiety and negativity. During the 21 days, it will be a conscious decision to self-improve every day, but after, it will be a habit and become a part of your authentic self, which will allow you to do it almost effortlessly.

You may still get anxious thoughts, but a rush of endorphins and positive thoughts will allow you to move on. With the completion of the Shadow Workbook comes clear a journey of self-improvement and a feeling of improved self-esteem. You can do this!

"Shadow work is the path
of the heart warrior".

INTRODUCTION TO CARL JUNG

Carl Jung was born on July 26th, 1875, and he was the founder of analytic psychology. His analytic psychology also included the study of the collective unconscious. He also studied the real correlation between illogical responses to stimulus words. He was able to find out that most mental illnesses were caused by emotionally charged clusters that could be attributed to unconsciousness. His finds were solidified by Freud's ideas, as they were contingent on one another on this account. Carl Jung's methods look to our shadows; he suggested that we have hidden anxieties and repressed thoughts. His methods of analysis strive to pull out the unconscious into the conscious in an attempt for self-improvement and being self-aware.

To the Shadow Workbook Content

This Shadow Workbook content endeavors to help reshape the readers' habits within 21 days to eliminate negativity and anxiety. "Why 21 days?", you may ask. According to Maxwell Maltz, it takes 21 days to change a habit: therefore, it's a 21-day challenge. The Shadow Workbook will talk about those possible habits that you want to change during your 21-day journey.

WHAT IS SHADOW WORK?

A few habits that you might want to change are, as mentioned: going to bed late, doing work while you eat, not taking time to relax each day, or even leaving stuff laying around instead of putting it away immediately. The daily reflection exercises can help you find the reason why you hold on to these bad habits and find it difficult to change them. Many people find it very hard to spend less time on social media and instead spend more time on themselves or in direct contact with people. Plus, with increased social media presence, it can occur almost an obsession with one's physical appearance and perceived shortcomings. Carl Jung suggested that it is necessary to know that all aspects of yourself, both subconscious and conscious, are fulfilled. In fact, Carl Jung believed that you could not change anything unless you first accepted it. By understanding the four main archetypes and following this 21-day plan, you too can change those bad habits and become self-aware.

Analyzing the Self archetype and all its parts daily is just one way you can become more self-aware. When you're talking to a coworker or friend, and they say something that evokes a feeling in you, stop and ask yourself why. If you have negative thoughts like "I can't do that," ask yourself, "Why can't I do that?" Maybe the reason you can't go to bed early enough is that you believe you haven't done enough or your desired achievements of the day were not reached. Go easy on yourself and look closely at what your hopes, desires, and beliefs are. Your personality is made up of those hopes and desires, but another aspect is your ego and unconscious mind. The ego has a few components, like the focus on survival, pleasure, perception of others, and desire for success or achievement. Your unconscious mind is composed of the unknown aspects of your personality. By identifying your conscious attributes, like your point of view, beliefs, feelings, and thoughts, you can explore the unconscious. With this Shadow Workbook 21-day plan, you can use the Self archetype to unearth why it's so difficult to put work aside and just eat your meal.

Unlike the inability to put work aside to eat, the compulsion to constantly be on social media can stem from an Anima or Animus. If there is an anomaly that others or you see as particular, personality may compel us to seek validation. While it more commonly presents itself in adolescents, a feminine or masculine physical characteristic that society or you have deemed to be an abnormality can compel us to get likes online. One look in a mirror may say there's a particular feature that is found unbecoming, and if that feature is excited on or constantly reminded of it, that becomes an Anima. Oftentimes, the Anima is created because of social norms or outside forces, and through self-assurance and daily reminders, this Anima will no longer be the driving force in our lives.

Carl Jung hit it right on the mark when he said, "the most terrifying thing is to accept oneself completely." It is also true that there is a sense of relief and confidence afterward. If your Anima resides more in your unconscious thoughts, it may result in repressed ideas. Those repressed thoughts or ideas are an aspect or component of your Shadow.

The Shadow is made up of a lot of attributes or components like weaknesses, desires, instincts, and maybe even perceived shortcomings. If your instincts tell you to just go and go without stopping, you could find yourself constantly taking things out and not putting them back. This behavior can stem from anxiety and feelings of shortcomings like you're not doing enough in the day or a subconscious deep desire to do more. One exercise you could do is taking a deep breath after finishing a task to slow down and then say to yourself, "I did a good job." The act of slowing down and taking one task at a time can help lower your anxiety while saying to yourself, "I did a good job" will help alleviate any anxiety about how the task was completed. The Workbook content aims to follow and look at each one of the four archetypes and analyze your reactions accordingly. This process will help find the target source and it will lead you to a solution.

What Are the Four Archetypes?

The four main archetypes are as listed: the Self, the Anima, the Persona, and the Shadow. Each of these four archetypes provides a specific exploration into your subconscious and authentic self. It is possible for them to appear overlapped, but this is only because your authentic self is deeply intertwined in each one of these four archetypes. As an example, one might alter their behavior because of the Anima and, in turn, modify their Persona accordingly. Following the modification, a distinct contrast between the Self and the Persona may occur, which causes anxiety and negativity. It's through the exploration of the Shadow that anyone can be allowed to identify these conflicts and imbalances within our authentic selves. That being said, let's begin the exploration of each one of these four archetypes so that you may better understand them and embark on your journey.

The Self archetype is an archetype that has fewer components and yet is the cornerstone to exploring the causes of someone's anxiety and negativity. The three components to exploring the self are your personality type, the ego, and the unconscious. The Self is created through the process that is known as individuation. Think of individuation as the various characteristics of the personality integrated into a separate thing when the personality and ego interact. Jung believed the imbalance between the subconscious and conscious is the cause of anxiety and negativity, which means the four archetypes must work in tangent with one another. To understand the Self, let's begin defining the ego and the personality.

The ego is a person's self-esteem and self-worth, while the personality is the characteristics or qualities that make up a person's character. That being said, you may be wondering how your character is affected by your self-esteem or self-worth. Knowing how one affects the other will allow you to analyze the creation of the Self, and through this exploration, you will be able to know your authentic self.

Another archetype in your authentic self is the Anima, and while it commonly resides in the conscience, when there is a conflict with the Self archetype, it can be pushed to the subconscious. When this happens, exploration becomes a necessity because of how the formation of anxiety and negativity can be created. The Anima corresponds to feminine attributes or characteristics, both physical and mental, that appear in a male. Whereas the Anima that appears within females corresponds to attributes or characteristics, both physical and mental, that are typically masculine. With a simple look in a full-body mirror, physical attributes or characteristics can be identified, which in term allow us to identify an obvious Anima. On the other hand, mental/psychological attributes or characteristics require self-reflection. If these mental/psychological attributes or characteristics have been pushed to the subconscious, the self-reflection may require lots of thinking and may result in some painful realizations. Carl Jung once said, though, "There's no coming to conscious without pain." In many cases, pain can be a good thing when used to motivate us to make progress. Our body's natural response to pain, however, tends to be to turn away from it because of societal norms that suppose that pain is a bad thing. The Persona archetype is created to protect us from it; knowing this, we can begin exploring it.

The Persona archetype is the person or persona we project outwardly to others or even characteristics and attributes we have that can be directly linked to society. When applying the Persona archetype to the endeavor of exploring our anxieties and negativity, it's helpful to observe our behavioral changes, even thoughts or feelings. When you are alone, does your behavior differ from when you are with family or friends? When answering this question, don't think about activities that you would participate in, but about mannerisms or how you carry yourself. When you're alone, do you slouch? When you're with your friends and family, do you sit up perfectly straight? If this applies to you, it's very possible that you become anxious about how you hold your body.

Say, for instance, that when you're around your family, they constantly correct your grammar; this could result in negative thoughts towards yourself like you're not smart enough. While this may not be true or even conscious, your subconscious mind could interpret those words as such. In this example, it would be to your benefit to remind yourself that you are smart and that you do have worth. Some may take the approach of just widening their vocabulary and brushing up on their English language skills. Either of these approaches is healthy and could result in the alleviation of anxiety and/or negativity. Keep in mind that the Shadow archetype plays a fundamental role in the creation of the Persona.

"How much do I keep in mind, though?", you may ask yourself. Well, the Shadow is composed of the following: repressed ideas or feelings, perceived weaknesses, desires, instincts, and shortcomings. When these aspects of the Shadow interact with the other archetypes, additional attributes or characteristics of the Shadow can form. These are envy, greed, prejudice, hate, and even aggression. When these additional characteristics or attributes form, they result in anxiety and negativity, which, if you wish to eliminate them, must be explored. For Carl Jung said, "We cannot change anything unless we accept it." As you may very well know, a crucial part of accepting something is that you know what that something is.

This Shadow Workbook will help you tap into your unconscious mind and show you just how powerful it is. You will learn about your triggers and why they occur. While using this Workbook, you will gain knowledge of the source of your anxiety and negativity. Your unconscious and inner child know the true source, and through the exploration of your authentic self, so will you. It will take a 21-day commitment, which is okay because you can do it!

Now you can do an exercise to explore these four main archetypes. To explore your Self archetype, reflect on your basic desires and what your body or mind instinctively wants. For this experience, ask yourself, "What can I do to feel more like myself and booster my self-esteem?" When exploring the Anima archetype, try looking at yourself in the mirror. As you may have seen on TV, bullies will shame people for being different. It's possible that you are doing this to yourself. The next step to this experience is to list five attributes, either physical or mental, that you like about yourself. Listing five ways you are different when you're not alone is a good way to explore the Persona archetype. Finally, it's time to explore your Shadow archetype by listing five perceived weaknesses or shortcomings.

Desires

1) _____

2) _____

3) _____

4) _____

5) _____

Self-esteem boosters

1) _____

2) _____

3) _____

4) _____

5) _____

Good attributes

1) _____

2) _____

3) _____

4) _____

5) _____

Ways I change

1) _____

2) _____

3) _____

4) _____

5) _____

Weaknesses or shortcomings

1) _____

2) _____

3) _____

4) _____

5) _____

After completing the exercise, you may begin to wonder what that accomplished or how that could help you. Fulfilling your desires is the path to feeling happier and feeling like you are getting the most out of life. If you are, you can be confident about your choices and not feel anxious about them or even negative. The choice to love yourself the way you are helps eliminate negative feelings towards yourself about how you look or act. When you list your good attributes, you also boost your self-esteem because you're focusing on the good things and not just on the bad ones. Too often, you focus on those because we are wired to do so to help us survive. Focusing on the bad things too much negatively impacts our lives, so it's important to adapt and change those tendencies to survive. That's why listing five ways you can change for the better is so beneficial. If there were no changes that you needed to make in your life, you wouldn't be feeling anxious or negative. One way to find possible changes that need to happen is by acknowledging your shortcomings and weaknesses. It's during these 21 days of exercises that you will be able to explore these lists more to eliminate your anxiety and negativity.

What Does the Shadow Workbook Accomplish?

During the 21 days of exercises within this Shadow Workbook, you will identify your triggers and accomplish the elimination of your anxiety and negativity. You'll be able to eliminate them by finding the sources of those triggers. After finding the sources, you can begin the process of making changes within your life that will ultimately eliminate your negativity and anxiety. It is also quite possible that by getting to know your authentic self/ shadow self, your anxieties and negativities will be eliminated. For some, strictly the understanding of "why" can do wonders.

MEETING YOUR SHADOW SELF!

The wonderful knowledge and the carefully constructed 21 days of exercises that lie within this Workbook are amazing. You will be able to really get to know your authentic/shadow self and, by doing so, eliminate your negativity and anxiety. The carefully constructed exercises will explore the four main archetypes that make up your shadow self. With these archetypes, your exploration will take a clear path. You will get to know your Shadow, Anima, Persona, and Self archetypes of yourself.

Why Analyze Your Shadow Self?

You may be saying, "why can't you just tell me what I am supposed to be doing? I'll do it." The answer to that is really not that simple because everyone has their unique analysis; humans are very complex. It's only through analyzing yourself and doing the daily exercises that you can begin to make the necessary changes. These are paramount for the elimination of your anxiety and negativity. At times, it may seem like only the bad things are surfacing, but remember that where it is bad, there is an equal amount of good. Good lies within everyone, and yes, that means you too. Maybe you're messing up a lot at work or with friends and you think that makes you a bad person. You can be wrong. Everyone messes up and needs to adjust how they are doing something if it's not working. All that is required to be a good person is to keep trying and remind us that we all make mistakes. Good lies within us all. If you feel like there isn't enough good residing. within yourself, this Workbook can help you find it. Reading it does more than just analyze mistakes and negative feelings. While on your journey, you will be exploring your inner child and getting to know your authentic self. Carl Jung believed no one is inherently good or bad, but it is our actions and the choices we make that make us so. You are endeavoring to improve yourself, and that choice reflects who you are as a person.

What Good Lies Within?

Carl Jung also said that getting to know your shadow self can not only help you understand the bad things that you are capable of, but also the good ones. To get to know the good that lies within, you must get to the root of your desires, hopes, and dreams. It is the unconscious mind, your authentic self, that is the driving force for your daily habits or even your desires. It really will help to discover your personal unconscious and to learn what makes you tick or what motivates you.

Knowing that good lies within you will also help you stay positive. Too often, we give up because we think it's hopeless, but the Shadow Workbook can show you that, actually, it's not hopeless at all. You can find the good that lies within you. When you see someone hurting, I'm sure you empathize with them, and it hurts you that they are in pain. It's indeed hard to find the good in yourself and have good self-esteem when you're getting anxious and negative all day, every day. That's why it's so important that you embark on your self-improvement journey to get to know your inner child.

Self-Esteem

It's very hard not to be anxious or negative when you don't appreciate your full self. With thoughts like, "I can never be a good spouse or parent," or even, "I'm too stupid to do anything right," you won't be able to eliminate your anxiety. It is crucial to love yourself, for only through caring and effort can change come about. You are worth caring about! The fact that you are reading this is evidence enough that you care about yourself and want to self-improve.

Will My Life Be Better for It?

Your life can get better by using this book, and in many different ways too. For starters, your relationships will improve because you'll have more mental energy to have fun.

Without that emotional anvil on your chest, you will have inner peace present in every second of the day. You'll be able to go out for a walk and fully take in every moment of the birds chirping or the wind on your face. Listening to your loved ones talk about their day will be fun and could be the highlight of your day again.

Can Using the Shadow Workbook Be Hard?

It is true: getting to a good point again won't be easy, but nothing worth obtaining is. Any time you self-reflect and look inwards, you could find something hard to deal with. It may take some time to look inside yourself, and with the world we live in, that can be hard. You know it's important to eliminate your anxiety and negativity. Inevitably, a change of any kind can be and is indubitably difficult, but it is worth it. And so it can be using The Shadow Workbook to eliminate your anxiety and negativity. While using this Workbook, you will be diving into repressed ideas and memories, so you'll need to deal with those feelings when they come to the surface. They were repressed because, at the time, your mind thought you couldn't process them, but they are still affecting you. It's imperative to remember you are stronger now. The hardness of those feelings will be replaced with life without anxiety and negativity once you process them. You can be happier by working through this hardship in the foreseeable future. The journey that you will embark on with this book is worth it.

The Exploration

In this book, you will go on an exploration of your psyche to discover the solution to eliminating your anxiety and negativity. While diving into your four archetypes, the Self, the Anima, the Shadow, and the Persona, you will find long-lost information about your inner child. With this knowledge, you will get to know your authentic self and find what can bring you joy within the hardship. You'll be able to answer questions like, "Why do I get so anxious when strangers talk to me at the store?"

While you will not have control over what you learn about yourself, it is crucial to do so. Although, after discovering what's within your unconscious, giving you a better understanding of yourself is important to continue your journey. It's not only important but necessary, as you are in an ongoing process of self-improvement. Don't expect perfection at any point in your journey because it is an unattainable goal, as perfection is subjective. You are on an ongoing journey on a path to self-improvement!

While you self-improve, it will be necessary for you to self-analyze. Self-analyzing is a key point in Carl Jung's method. He said, "knowing your own darkness is the best method for dealing with the darkness of other people." It's the confidence and self-assurance within ourselves that allows us to have the strength to deal with everyday life.

While it's true the journey to self-improvement is not easy, because getting to know yourself may be painful, he also said, "There's no coming to consciousness without pain." He knew that things reside within our unconscious minds for a reason, and while the healing process is needed to bring it to the conscious, it is painful. Your mind can never repress anything fully, so though you may not be aware of the source of your anxiety and negativity, your brain does know. The good news is you don't have to be what happens to you, but what you choose to become; Carl Jung also believed this.

During your exploration, you will be endeavoring to pull your unconscious mind into your conscious mind. To bring your unconscious mind forward, you will need to look deeper into your own self and soul. Carl Jung said: "your visions will become clear only when you look into yourself and self-reflect on any possible meanings". It is now your goal to do just that and look into your heart. Go forward and self-analyze every aspect of your life, both small and big. He believed that there were no irrelevant aspects of our lives. Begin your journey by observing your life and self-analyzing.

The Analysis of Myself

While on this journey to self-improvement, you will be expected to analyze yourself. While using the Workbook to analyze yourself and by using the exercises, you will be able to identify target problems, which will give you the ability to postulate a solution. Below are possible problems that may be found after exploring your authentic self with this Workbook and could be the source of anxiety or negativity. Also listed below are possible solutions for things that can be changed to help eliminate problems and the corresponding anxiety or negativity.

How Do You Do Self Analysis?

The first thing you'll do is to identify a problem that's consciously causing you anxiety or negativity. Next, really think about your authentic self and how the four archetypes could be the unconscious source. Finally, you will be capable of devising a solution, which could consist of a change in perspective or a behavior change. Now that you are aware of all the steps, you may be wondering, "Well, how do I identify the problem or conscious cause of my anxiety and negativity?"

You identify a problem by listening to your body and observing its reactions to your surroundings. Some possible reactions are tightness of the chest or hypervigilance; both are evidence that you're feeling anxious or negative. An example of a surrounding you may be in is a crowded room or alone in your home. It's only after you identify that there is a problem that you can meditate on what it could be about. Thoughts will cross your mind, and once you have identified what the problem is, your symptoms will subside a little. Your brain knows that identifying the problem is the first step to eliminating the issue.
Now that you have found out what the problem is, you can use the four archetypes to determine what the cause actually is. As stated before, the four archetypes are the Shadow, the Self, the Anima, and the Persona.

If the problem is you get anxious when you're at home alone and feel negative about yourself, we can begin to postulate. The Shadow archetype could quite possibly desire lots of human interaction or large amounts of stimuli. The Self might believe that not having people around you or people to talk to must mean you are undesirable. The Anima may think that society says we need to be around people, and not being around people means there's something wrong. While, on the other hand, the Persona could be out of balance because you give an outward appearance of being a people person. People persons have people to hang out with, and if you do not, that disrupts the Persona you have displayed.

If these archetypes conflict with one another and they are not all working in tangent, the solution is obvious. It is paramount that you begin to hang out and talk to people regularly. Don't think about it as if your mental health relies solely on others, but that you like being around people and can't deny that part of yourself. On the other hand, if you find that your four archetypes were against each other, that is evidence of a deeper personal imbalance. If this is happening, then it's possible you are denying who you are as a person. Just because society says you should want to be around people doesn't mean you necessarily have to. The same can be said if a part of you wants to be around people, but another part says that you'll get hurt, so you shouldn't want to. Life is not worth living without there being some risk, and it's okay to get sometimes hurt as long as we pick ourselves back up again. Here are some other possible problems and solutions following the Carl Jung method.

POSSIBLE PROBLEMS AND SOLUTIONS

Problem #1
Being in Public Makes Me Anxious

Possible Authentic Self Realizations

- **The Shadow:** Within my subconscious resides the idea that I must stay home, for home is my safe place. My desires and wants have put my home as a good place more than anywhere else. Given the fact that I have been hurt while not at home, I desire to stay away from that potential pain.

- **The Self:** My ego/self-esteem was damaged when I was in public due to bullying and the inability to have the same mannerisms as others. My personality dictates that I hold my head high and defend others in their time of need. How am I supposed to hold my head high or defend others when I feel unable to do so?

- **The Anima:** My mannerisms are more masculine, and others find them to be confrontational. Being that I am not a confrontational person and my personality is quite warm and loving of others, I am facing a conflict within myself.

- **The Persona:** Due to repressed trauma out in public, my Persona in public is confrontational and adversarial. My authentic self has changed my Persona in this way as a coping mechanism to protect myself.

Changes I Can Make

I must confront my trauma and remind myself that it's okay to grieve so that I may alleviate my anxiety and/or negativity. Carl Jung said, "I am not what happened to me; I am what I choose to become." With this fact, I can also remind myself that lightning never strikes twice in the same place. By processing my trauma, my mannerisms may in fact, change. If they do not, that would be fine too because I can remember that my authentic self is one that protects me. Inside my ego is a person that knows I'm worth protecting; therefore, I should be proud of my mannerisms. As for my Persona, a mere explanation to those around me that I care about could alleviate any conflicts. With the absence of conflicts with others, I could alleviate the conflict within myself, and in turn, alleviate my anxiety and negativity.

Problem #2
I Don't Like the Way I Look

Possible Authentic Self Realizations

- **The Shadow:** I desire to shine, and while it may be an immature desire, it is a part of who I am. It's important not to repress this desire and to live life to my fullest, so I will accept this desire as a part of my authentic self. One of my shortcomings is that I often put others' desires before my own.

- **The Self:** My ego suffers when I let others' desires before my own. My personality dictates that I persevere and follow my instincts to live for who I am without reprieve. To live for myself and follow my desires unapologetically is my authentic self, and I acknowledge that only by doing so can I eliminate my anxieties and negativity. My Self does not allow others to dictate who I am.

- **The Anima:** I prefer short hair, but short hair is for boys.

- **The Persona:** I think things as efficiently as possible, and I feel like having long hair isn't efficient because it takes more maintenance.

Changes I Can Make

The first thing I can change is to wear the shining jewelry and accessories that I like proudly. I will remind myself that these are the things that my authentic self likes, and to live for myself to the fullest I must let my Self be happy with them. The next thing I will do is cut my hair short and let everyone close to me know that I love my hair and it expresses who I am on the inside. I will remind myself that if people really cared about me, they wouldn't want me to be anxious or not about how I look. In addition, I would tell myself this is who I am, and it's a good thing to show it to the world.

Problem #3
When People Come Over to My House, I Have Anxiety and Worry About What They'll Think

Possible Authentic Self Realizations

- **The Shadow:** I desire others' approval to reinforce that I am doing a good job. One of my repressed ideas is that because of my upbringing, I don't have the necessary skills to make a good home. While I have the desire, like many others, to do so because of my instinct to have a warm and inviting home, I often doubt myself. It's fair to say that I even envy others that were brought up in a way that taught them how to make a warm and inviting home.

- **The Self:** My self-esteem is hinged on others' approval of my actions and accomplishments. This can be directly linked to my personality's tendency to need others around because I am an extrovert.

- **The Anima:** I find inter design difficult, and often my sense of taste does not align with social norms. A typical female characteristic is the ability to belong and interact within a village of people. My Anima is such that I gravitate more towards groups of three or four because I desire a more personal interaction. My anxieties and negativity come to a head when I have gatherings because, more often than not, they are all larger than I desire. I do this because I think it matters that everyone can find their small three or four people they can interact with.

- **The Persona:** Sometimes, I project the person I believe I'm supposed to be and not the person I am to gain acceptance or approval from those I care about. My Persona represents me as a well-adjusted female that is also an experienced hostess.

Changes I Can Make

With the realizations that I have made and in the name of being my authentic self, I would first remind myself that if I'm not happy, no one can be happy when they come over. People know when you are anxious or stressed, and they tend to feel those same feelings too, out of empathy. Next, I would remind myself that it's my home, and if I'm happy with it, others that truly care about me will also be happy with it. My Anima makes me special, and so my next step would be reminding myself I am cherished and loved for who I am, not for what I do. When people come over to my home, I will choose to see me and not my stuff. Finally, I could become more well-adjusted and learn more about hosting by observing others. It's also within my power to read up on the topic beforehand and ask others for feedback the next time.

NOW YOU!

Problem:

_____

Possible Authentic Self-Realizations:

The Shadow _____

_____

_____

_____

_____

The Self _____

_____

_____

_____

_____

The Anima _____

_____

_____

_____

_____

The Persona _____

_____

_____

_____

_____

Solution:

_____

_____

_____

_____

_____

_____

_____

_____

_____

_____

_____

_____

_____

_____

_____

_____

_____

_____

_____

Problem:

_____

Possible Authentic Self-Realizations:

The Shadow _____

_____

_____

_____

_____

The Self _____

_____

_____

_____

_____

The Anima _____

_____

_____

_____

_____

The Persona _____

_____

_____

_____

_____

Solution:

_____

_____

_____

_____

_____

_____

_____

_____

_____

_____

_____

_____

_____

_____

_____

_____

_____

_____

Problem:

_____

Possible Authentic Self-Realizations:

The Shadow _____

_____

_____

_____

_____

The Self _____

_____

_____

_____

_____

The Anima _____

_____

_____

_____

_____

The Persona _____

_____

_____

_____

_____

Solution:

_____

_____

_____

_____

_____

_____

_____

_____

_____

_____

_____

_____

_____

_____

_____

_____

_____

_____

Exercise Explanation

Doing this exercise will help you find the source of the problem. You are endeavoring to learn more about your inner child, comprised of these four main archetypes. While you keep that problem in mind, keep these four main archetypes in mind too, to analyze yourself healthily. It's only so that your analysis of self-improvement can occur.

Why? How Will This Help Me?

If you understand the source of your problem, you can work to eliminate your anxiety and negativity. Doing so will enable you to find some inner peace. Going through each day with a weight on your chest is exhausting. Your days will be much more enjoyable if you're not weighed down by your anxiety and negativity.

MUST DO'S!

Keeping an open mind is key for all these exercises and for any progress to be made. If you think there's no more you can learn about yourself, then there won't be anything more you will learn about yourself. You know that there's a problem and that improvement needs to be made, or you wouldn't be reading this book. Now you have to say to yourself that it's okay and that we're all on our own journey. Next, have clean intentions while reading every word and doing your Shadow Plan. The more goal-oriented you are, the higher the probability that you will achieve your goal. To do so, you must also be consistent because this allows behavioral changes. If your brain has an oath not to change, it most definitely will not, because who likes to change? Changes are uncomfortable. To eliminate your negativity and anxiety, you must be determined and unwavering. So, let's begin your journey of self-improvement and identify those triggers.

What Are Triggers?

When we think about triggers, we think about emotional responses, and that would be correct. A trigger is a cause of an event or situation you are in. Given that the issue at hand is anxiety and negativity, we can conclude that the event or situation you are in is being anxious and/or negative. These feelings alert you through a trigger, and only through observing your environment can you know what that trigger is. A possible trigger could be being in a loud, crowded room or people watching you eat. The thing triggering you could be either conscious or unconscious. The point of this Shadow Workbook and constructing a Shadow Plan is to identify the triggers.

Possible Triggers

A possible trigger that you could identify is having anxiety about being alone at home and not talking to anyone. It could be that you don't have object permanence and that not having someone right there gives you the feeling that you have no one. Another possibility is that you're triggered by people watching you eat. One of the reasons why this might trigger you is because you are self-conscious about how you look. Making a purchase, even for something that's a necessity, could make you anxious and be a trigger. If you grew up not having enough or feel like those around you make much more than you do, this could be the cause of your trigger. Once you identify your triggers, healing can begin.

To begin the journey of removing your anxieties and negativity, the first step is to identify triggers to analyze your authentic self within your subconscious. Once we know the triggers, we can begin the process of analyzing them to find their root and ultimately alleviate anxiety or negativity. For your first full day using this Shadow Workbook, pay attention to how things make you feel. Whenever you feel anxious, take up your Workbook and document the event for later reflection. If there aren't enough spots, that's okay because you can use a blank sheet of paper and answer the same questions listed below. Let's begin the first step...

EXERCISE: TRIGGER LOG

Trigger Alert!!!

What Triggered You:

_____

_____

_____

_____

Who Triggered You:

_____

_____

_____

_____

How Did You Feel:

_____

_____

_____

_____

When Did It Happen:

_____

_____

_____

_____

Where Were You:

_____
_____
_____
_____

Extra Notes:

_____
_____
_____
_____
_____
_____
_____
_____
_____
_____
_____
_____
_____
_____
_____
_____
_____
_____

Trigger Alert!!!

What Triggered You:

_____

_____

_____

_____

Who Triggered You:

_____

_____

_____

_____

How Did You Feel:

_____

_____

_____

_____

When Did It Happen:

_____

_____

_____

_____

Where Were You:

_____

_____

_____

_____

Extra Notes:

_____

_____

_____

_____

_____

_____

_____

_____

_____

_____

_____

_____

_____

_____

_____

_____

_____

_____

Trigger Alert!!!

What Triggered You:

_____
_____
_____
_____

Who Triggered You:

_____
_____
_____
_____

How Did You Feel:

_____
_____
_____
_____

When Did It Happen:

_____
_____
_____
_____

Where Were You:

_____

_____

_____

_____

Extra Notes:

_____

_____

_____

_____

_____

_____

_____

_____

_____

_____

_____

_____

_____

_____

_____

_____

_____

TRIGGER REFLECTION

Think about your triggers impact your daily behaviors. Are there things you avoid or don't like to do because you're afraid they might trigger you? How do you try to recover after you've been triggered?

_____

_____

_____

_____

_____

_____

_____

_____

_____

_____

_____

_____

_____

_____

_____

_____

_____

_____

_____

Exercise Explanation

Completing this exercise will enable you to be more aware of the specific things that trigger you. A person that used to be famous once said, "Knowing is half the battle." That's why answering what, when, where, and how can allow you to analyze the trigger. The extra notes section is for your thoughts and self-reflection on the trigger in question. Your trigger may not be obvious at first because of the overwhelming feelings that may be clouding it.

It's possible that talking to people makes you anxious because you're worried about how they will react to what you said. It is equally possible that you look up to someone and you're afraid of messing up in front of them. Even having negative thoughts about your choice at lunch could stem from a past of bad eating habits. That is why you must answer all the questions with great thought and effort.

Why? How Will This Help?

"Why must I put great thought and effort into answering these questions?" you may ask. The answer to that is quite simple. Only through deep contemplation can you truly find what's actually triggering you. Sometimes, our triggers like to play peekaboo and only briefly reveal themselves to us. By answering these questions and participating fully in the exercise, you will be able to identify your trigger honestly.

Analyzing Your Triggers

Looking back on your day, how did these triggers affect your behavior throughout the day? First, organize your triggers from "it completely changed my day" to "I barely remembered what happened." Can the ones that affected you the most be avoided? Could telling someone about the trigger alleviate it? If there are triggers that you barely remember, why did they affect you so much at the time? What did or could you do to turn your day back around after you have been triggered?

Write down all the answers to these questions below along with why you think you are triggered.

_____

_____

_____

_____

_____

_____

_____

_____

_____

_____

_____

Now that you have completed today's exploration of yourself, try and do some self-care or do some extra things that are right for you. After an emotional endeavor, it's important to recharge your emotional batteries. After completing an exercise like the trigger log, try doing something like taking a bubble bath or going for a walk in the woods. Do just about anything that brings you joy and recharges your emotional batteries. Keeping them as full as possible will make the process of eliminating your anxiety and negativity significantly easier.

OUR REALITY

Carl Jung said our inner child is formed through the interaction of the world around us and those in it. Your reality is not only the people that are closest to you but also the things they say to you and what you perceive them to have done to you. While we create our reality at the basic level with our five senses, there is a whole other level to reality.

This other level of our reality is created within our mind and is done through what we perceive others to have done. We use a method called cause and effect to establish the attributes of all four of our archetypes. For example, if someone with a space in between their two top buck teeth made a high-pitched sound every time they talked, and other people laughed, that would be the cause. The inevitable effect would be that they felt uncomfortable being laughed at and would hate their teeth. What you do at that moment will cement what type of person you are. At this moment, you want to eliminate your negativity and anxiety. You know the effect it's having on your life right now, but the question is what in your reality is causing it. One way to alleviate the causes of your anxiety and negativity is to find out what affects them. You have learned about triggers, so let's explore your reality to understand your conscience and subconscious self better.

An Exploration Into Your Self

It's another day, and you have officially committed to completing all 21 days of self-exploration into your authentic self. Now that you have identified some triggers, the next thing to do is to get to know your shadow self. To get to know it, and ultimately your authentic self, it's important to put everything on the table. Jung believed that all people are made up of three different parts, which are the ego, the personal unconscious, and the collective unconscious.

The Ego

The ego is quite simply your conscious self and what you can consider to be you. When someone says that a person has a big ego, they are saying that person is full of themselves. If you wake up every morning and do your self-care, a part of your ego cares about your appearance. Exploring the four major archetypes can help you understand why that exactly is. Another possible characteristic of your ego could be that you are eco-conscious. If you are very eco-conscious, then you might wear hemp clothes or might use animal cruelty-free products. Both examples are possible characteristics of your ego.

The Personal Unconscious

On the other hand, the personal unconscious is the repressed ideas or memories that lie within the mind. They have been put off to the side, and they are an instrumental aspect of who you are. The memories or ideas that lie within your personal unconscious must be accessed to make any self-improvement. An example of personal traumatic memories that may have been repressed from your childhood would be if you were attacked by a dog. Well, it's possible you don't remember being attacked by a dog, but it happened; therefore, it affects you. These repressed ideas or memories are just one reason why sharing this Workbook with others in your life may be helpful. You could meditate to bring these memories to the surface, or you could also talk to those around you who would remember and know them.

The Collective Unconscious

The collective unconscious won't be so easy to access. These are repressed impulses or beliefs. Some examples of your collective unconscious in your daily life may be the feeling of déjà vu or even love at first sight. Even something such as being afraid of monsters can be a part of it because of society. The collective unconscious mind is rooted in the idea that our culture inevitably shapes who we are as a person. One exercise you can do to fully explore your reality is to write on the line the first thing that comes to mind.

EXERCISE: WHO AM I?

My name is _____. I am _____ years old, and I spend my spare time _____. I also love to _____, _____, _____, and _____.

These are just a few things that allow my authentic self to shine and give me happiness. I am a good person and I know myself better than anyone.

Three words that I would use to describe myself are _____, _____, and _____. I am a good _____and I'm great at _____. I love that I can _____, _____, and _____ well. Someday I want to_____.

One of my dreams is to _____ _____. I would like to go on a trip with _____. Some other important people to me are _____, _____, and _____.

Three things that I have done that I'm proud of are _____, _____, and _____. After doing those things I felt _____ and _____. I can feel that same way after completing daily essential tasks like _____, _____, and _____. If the tiniest of mistakes matter, then so do the tiniest of victories, and getting up in the morning every day and keeping going is a tiny victory.

Was there ever a time when you met someone and just knew instantly if you were going to like them or not? Circle Yes or No.

Something that scares me is _____. When I was a kid, some of the things that I did to pass the time were _____, _____, _____, and _____.

Exercise Explanation

Your ego is made up of your desires and other things that you consider a part of who you are. This exercise made you list some of these desires and things that are part of you. After doing this exercise, you got to know your ego just a little bit more. Getting to know every possible aspect of yourself allows you to find target areas that need improvement. It's very possible that your ego is in check and that it's your unconscious where the issue lies.

This exercise also allowed you to get to know your personal unconscious by thinking back to your childhood. We often don't think about memories from our childhood as they are repressed. While doing this exercise, you had to think back to that time and therefore explore your personal unconscious. You had to think about either a time when you were most happy or a time when you were miserable. Whichever the case may be, it allowed you to explore an aspect of yourself that may be out of balance and need some self-reflection.

Your collective unconscious, however, entails more of a societal aspect. When we think back to what we did as children, we often realize that many other people the same age did the same things. That is because what we did as children is what society says children should be doing. When listing off essential daily tasks, you begin to realize that it is also the society that tells us that those are essential daily tasks, and we do them without thinking. The reason is that they are a part of our collective unconscious.

Why? How Will This Help?

This exercise helps you to understand your ego, your personal unconscious, and your collective unconscious to know yourself better. It's only after reviewing the blueprints of how and why something works that anyone can see where something is going wrong. The fact that we need to review the blueprints could be why we are so curious and love a good mystery. People naturally want to know how, and this exercise helps you explore just that. Go forward and analyze yourself.

Moving Forward

First, you learned how to use the four main archetypes to analyze the source of a problem. After linking the source to a problem, you can devise a solution for going forward and ultimately eliminating the problem. The second thing you did was to identify your triggers, which are the emotional responses your unconscious was giving you to alert you of a problem. After analyzing your triggers, you were able to devise what the problem ultimately really was. Now, moving forward, you can repeat these two exercises daily to help eliminate any anxiety or negativity that surfaces. It's the third thing that you did, which was to do the exercise to understand your reality, that will ultimately give you a further understanding of your authentic self/ shadow self. The next step would be to go a bit further and explore your four main archetypes deeper.

The Self

This archetype is the part of our personality that interacts directly with our ego. The Self lies within the center of our personality and is surrounded by three other things. These three things that surround the Self are your consciousness, your ego, and your unconscious mind. They interact with the Self and are what give it life.

Your consciousness is composed of your points of view, beliefs, feelings, and thoughts. The source of why they exist is directly linked to the four main archetypes. It's the interaction of your consciousness, the ego, and the subconscious that make the self what it is. While they are interacting, aspects of your personality are formed. The ego, on the other hand, is formed from the moment of birth.

Your ego is your desire for survival, pleasure, success, achievements, or power. On our most basic primal level, we all want to stay to live another day. Even on our darkest days, filled with despair, we seek pleasure and to feel good. No matter how bad things get, your ego won't let you give up and wallow in your anxiety or negativity. Your ego desires success and achievement. It even searches for any level of power or control it can get its hands on because that's the way we are wired.

Your unconsciousness is all the aspects of your ego and your consciousness, but the ones that you're not aware of. The desire for power and control may be discussed with you; therefore, it gets repressed and it becomes an aspect of your unconsciousness. It's crucial to keep in mind that the fact that you repressed something does not make it go away. When dealing with anxiety or negativity, you might try to repress or overshadow these feelings. Pressing these feelings may give the appearance that you're not feeling them, but you are. All things that you repressed become a part of your unconscious mind and will indubitably affect you. To self-improve yourself, it is best to confront all aspects of yourself and repress nothing, or at least as much as you can.

The Shadow

Other things you may have repressed are ideas you may have had. All repressed ideas become a characteristic of your Shadow archetype. Along with repressed ideas are your weaknesses, desires, instincts, and shortcomings. Exploring this archetype will allow you to be your full self, both good and bad. It's only through acknowledging and working on our shortcomings that we can be our best selves. It's important to bring anything repressed to the surface during this self-exploration during the Shadow Plan.

Some possible repressed ideas might be that you should stop being someone's friend, and it would emerge through illogical irritation with them. You might not want to be this person's friend because they don't put the same amount of effort into the relationship as you. Because it doesn't seem realistic, you repress it, even though it quite possibly could be very healthy. Another possible repressed idea is about all the different types of desserts you want to bake and eat. You know that eating a lot of them is bad; therefore, you repress the idea. The good thing is that once this repressed idea comes to the surface, you can execute it with moderation. It is quite healthy to try a new baking recipe every weekend or every other weekend. While bringing these repressed ideas to the surface, it is important to acknowledge your weaknesses as well.

If you know that after baking a cake, you will eat all of it because it is one of your weaknesses, you can plan accordingly. If eating too many desserts is a weakness, you can invite friends over to share your cake with you after you bake it. By knowing you're going to share the cake with others, you conquer your weakness. Another possible weakness could be that you get easily bored; therefore, you find it difficult to do the repetitive tasks of the day. Once you know this is a weakness, then you can endeavor to make them more interesting by listening to music or doing multiple tasks at once. Another way to conquer a weakness is by rewarding yourself with one of your desires.

A desire that you could reward yourself with is a nice treat like a candy bar or a Caesar salad. When eating foods that you like, your body releases pleasure hormones as well anytime you indulge your desires. When you hang out with your friends and you're laughing and having a good time, pleasure hormones are also released, as you dive into this desire. If you find physical activities pleasurable because of this desire, your body will also release pleasure hormones. Knowing this, one can conclude that anything our body releases pleasure hormones for is one of our desires. Our body does this through instinct to incentivize us to do things that we like.

Instincts play an important role in our daily lives, as well as the Shadow archetype. Jung believed that there were five basic human instincts, and they were as follows: creativity, reflection, activity, sexuality, and hunger. Creativity is defined as the ability to create things that are original; we all have a desire for this. This instinct may emerge through the desire for children or through the simple aspiration to create art. Instead, the instinct for reflection can emerge through the belief in one's soul or desire to express thoughts and feelings. Moreover, your instinct for activity is merely a desire for work to help your society or group of people. Finally, sexuality as an instinct is not so easily explained, because it has many components. It can be your desire for another human being or how your specific sex fits in within society. Wanting to eat and craving to devour both knowledge and sustenance is another basic instinct. All of these instincts are characteristic of your Shadow archetype as well as any perceived shortcomings.

You may find yourself physically not as fit as others, and that might be a perceived shortcoming. It's also possible that you don't learn concepts as fast as others, which could be another example. While it is true that an abundance of perceived shortcomings can lead to anxiety and negativity, it is important to know why you view them as such. Your anxiety and negativity may be a direct result of a problem within your unconscious mind. Whether they hold true or not, shortcomings are characteristic of your Shadow archetype. Therefore, all proceed shortcomings must be addressed and/or faced.

Other things you must face are any feelings of envy, greed, prejudice, or hate you may have. These feelings cloud and taint the Shadow archetype, and you must face and overcome them for the purpose of self-improvement. Having these characteristics will undoubtedly create negativity and anxiety because of the imbalance within yourself.

Many of these characteristics may indeed reside in your unconscious, which results in difficulty facing and overcoming them. If they are within your unconscious mind, they will emerge in your dreams or possibly even visions. These characteristics could even come out as unusual feelings during an event or occurrence of some kind. While you classify them as atypical, they are occurring for a reason, and through self-reflection or exploration of your authentic self, those reasons will become apparent.

The Anima

The Anima archetype is also apparent and easily explored. Anything that you see, or others see about yourself that is an anomaly becomes a part of the Anima archetype. While it's true that we live in an age of enlightenment, it is also true that we have certain characteristics that decidedly are male and female. If we display characteristics of the opposite sex that we believe we should have, it becomes a part of our Anima archetype. Something as simple as an extraordinarily tall female can be a part of the Anima archetype. Because of this anomaly, we will compensate and behave differently, whether we are doing it consciously or subconsciously. Really, any social influences that counter our self-image can also be a part of our Anima archetype.

Some social influences that might counter your self-image might be that you're a bigger male and dress like you're tough, and you don't have strong emotions. There is no direct link between someone's size and how they dress or between how someone dresses and how they feel. Despite that, society has created stereotypes, and it is those stereotypes that shape your Anima archetype. Society also helps shape your Persona archetype, except this archetype is there to protect us from stereotypes.

The Persona

The mask we wear around our family and friends is to meet standards and to give off an outward appearance that we meet those standards. We will look people in the eyes when we're talking to them so that they feel heard. It doesn't matter that we saw something out of the corner of our eye that we want to look at. The Persona archetype compels us to make our friends and family feel heard by making eye contact. When you're planning to go to a party, you will inevitably take extra care of your hygiene. You're what the Persona archetype dictates because everyone else will do this, so you must do it as well to fit in and meet the standard. Even if our desire is to let loose and just go in something nice, we will be compelled not to. Your Persona that you show to others will not allow you to do anything else without feeling anxious or having negative thoughts towards yourself.

EXERCISE: MY FOUR MAIN ARCHETYPES!

Think about a time when you were anxious or negative and use the four main archetypes to postulate why that may be. List one or two things about your Self, Shadow, Anima, and Persona archetypes below.

THE SELF

1) _____
   _____
2) _____
   _____

THE SHADOW

1) _____
   _____
2) _____
   _____

THE ANIMA

1) _____
   _____
2) _____
   _____

THE PERSONA

1) _____
   _____
2) _____
   _____

Exercise Explanation

Doing this exercise will help you analyze your negativity and/or your anxiety. The four main archetypes or the cause of a problem can be a tool for you. Knowing your authentic self is the only way to do any self-improvement. Analyzing your desires will allow you to see where they're not being fulfilled. If you know where your perceived shortcomings are, you can adjust accordingly. After completing this exercise, you can construct a plan to eliminate both your negativity and your anxiety.

Why? How Will This Help?

The source of your negativity and your anxiety can only be found through self-analysis. If you want to not feel anxiety, you must eliminate what you're anxious about. If you want to stop feeling so negative about yourself, you must know why. You can construct a plan only after you have all the information. This exercise allows you to obtain that very information.

Keep It Positive

While doing all of this self-analysis and exercises, it's important to stay positive, so doing a gratitude exercise would be advisable. There are things that you can say to yourself to stay positive. As well as positive, there are actions that you can do that will help keep yourself positive and recharge your emotional batteries. It can be helpful for you to stay positive to start off the day with an uplifting statement. It can also be beneficial to have a mantra that you repeat to yourself throughout the day.

Things You Can Say

Something you can tell yourself once you wake up is, "It's a new day, and it's going to be a good one!" This allows you to start over and get away from anything that might be bringing you down from the day before. Saying this is going to give you motivation. You could also say to yourself throughout the day, "I am strong, and I can do this!"

Reminding yourself that you are strong affirms that you are strong enough to conquer anything and that you can achieve your goal. Saying, "You can do this," reinforces what you already know in your heart. We all need reminders, which is why doing this enables you to reach your goal.

Things That You Can Do

Reminders can be very helpful, but after you remind yourself that you can do it, you got to do it. Doing exercises to keep yourself positive gives you the energy and motivation to get things done. Going for an occasional walk in the woods can help you see the beauty in the world and show that it's worth it to keep going. It's easy to get caught up in all the negativity in the world, and a beautiful reminder that there's still good in it can be beneficial. Text someone that you're close to and have a nice conversation. In the morning, drink a cup of coffee and focus on every sip and the warmth when it touches your tongue. Being in each moment and cherishing every second that you enjoy is yet another thing that you can do to remain positive. If you're up for it, think back to a time when things were worse and cherish where you are now. Even doing a gratitude exercise every 2 to 3 days can help keep you positive and motivated to continue your self-improvement journey.

Here is a gratitude exercise that you could try. The first thing you do is take a deep breath and clear your mind. Then, try to think of ten things that you are grateful for and you feel like they are making your life better. Write down something that brings you joy and that you're thankful that you have. Is there someone in your life that's really been there for you? Write down the name of the person that's been there for you. You could even be grateful for an experience that you had; it helped you.

EXERCISE: GRATITUDE

List 15 things that you are grateful for:

1) _____

2) _____

3) _____

4) _____

5) _____

7) _____

8) _____

9) _____

10) _____

11) _____

12) _____

13) _____

14) _____

15) _____

A LOVELY THING

Write more about one of the things from your gratitude list, and dig into the ways this thing makes your life better.

_____

_____

_____

_____

_____

_____

_____

_____

_____

_____

_____

_____

_____

_____

_____

_____

_____

_____

_____

_____

Exercise Explanation

Writing down the things that you are grateful for will bring them to the forefront of your mind. While it's true that unconsciously, you are always thankful for them, it's important to bring them to your conscious mind. Sometimes we just need a reminder of things that we are grateful for so that we can feel the joy. Life can get in the way, and we can get consumed by our anxiety or negativity. This exercise helps push those feelings aside so that we can feel grateful again.

Why? How Will This Help Me?

After this exercise, you should feel a sense of joy and happiness. Even a moment of relief from our anxiety or negativity is beneficial. This exercise helps give you a break from feeling your anxiety or negativity. Hold on to this feeling of happiness and let it motivate you to eliminate your anxiety and negativity.

GETTING READY TO USE THE WORKBOOK

You have already chosen to make those self-improvements and eliminate your anxiety or negativity. The next step is to get into the right mindset for self-improvement, and for eliminating those feelings. Complete your Shadow Plan with an open mind and be curious about yourself. There is hope, so be optimistic that you will succeed. You can do it. Believe, truly believe, that you will be able to do this, and you will. Remember, there are things that not even you know about yourself. Don't be afraid to explore the unknown about yourself and have your point of view changed.

When you're beginning, your journey of self-improvement is a good idea to have clear goals and know where you want to end up. Keep a clear goal in mind while doing your Shadow Plan. It can be helpful to imagine what your life will be like without any anxiety or negativity. That's why doing this Dear Future Me exercise can really help you know what your clear goal is.

EXERCISE: DEAR FUTURE ME

Write a workbook entry detailing things you want your future self to have. Consider what your future will look like without any anxiety or negativity. Don't be afraid to be ambiguous and optimistic with your vision. Being a dreamer and wanting things for yourself allows you to get more out of life.

Dear Future Me,

_____

_____

_____

_____

_____

_____

_____

_____

_____

_____

_____

_____

_____

_____

_____

_____

_____

_____

Sincerely Myself Now,

_____

_____

_____

_____

_____

_____

_____

_____

Exercise Explanation

Writing a letter to your future self allows you to imagine where you can be. Looking into the future can help you realize what your goals are and where you want to go. Doing this exercise will also help affirm that you can get there. You are on an ongoing journey and knowing that there is hope at the end waiting for you helps keep you motivated.

Why? How Will This Help Me?

You can't make any progress if you think you can't. You also can't eliminate that anxiety or negativity if you can't imagine life without it. Completing this exercise helps you imagine just that. It also helps you make your dream a reality because to get instructions during your journey, you need to have a destination.

AFFIRMATIONS FOR SHADOW INTEGRATION

SHADOW AFFIRMATIONS

Integrating the parts of ourselves that we have rejected or hidden can be a challenging and painful process, but it can also be incredibly liberating. When we accept all aspects of ourselves, including those that make us feel vulnerable or insecure, we can feel more whole and complete. The following affirmations can help support your shadow integration process and help you develop a loving and compassionate attitude towards yourself.

Before delving into the affirmations, it is important to understand how they can help with shadow integration. These affirmations are designed to help you:

• Accept and integrate all parts of yourself, including those that you may have rejected or hidden in the past.

• Develop a positive and empowering mindset that supports your growth and transformation.

• Replace old patterns of thought and behavior with new, healthier ones.

Self-Love

- *I am worthy of love and acceptance, regardless of my imperfections.*

- *I love and accept myself fully, with all my parts.*

- *I am the source of my love and happiness, and I give myself permission to cultivate them within me.*

- *I choose to love myself unconditionally, without judgment or criticism.*

- *I give myself permission to heal past wounds and love myself again.*

Self-Confidence

- I am secure and confident in myself, regardless of the challenges that may arise.

- I give myself permission to explore new experiences and make positive choices in my life.

 -I am able to make conscious decisions and trust my instincts.

- I am able to overcome my fears and face challenges with courage and determination.

- I give myself permission to follow my heart and pursue my dreams, even if they seem unreasonable.

Shadow Acceptance

- I welcome my shadow as part of me and integrate it into my life.

- I am able to accept my negative emotions without judgment or criticism.

- I give myself permission to explore my less-known sides and accept them without fear.

- I am able to see the beauty and value in all parts of myself, including those I may have rejected in the past.

- I accept my vulnerability and fragility as part of my humanity.

Emotional Healing

- I am able to heal from past emotional wounds and let them go.

- I give myself permission to freely express my emotions and accept them as part of me.

- I am able to forgive myself and others for any past mistakes.

- I welcome my sadness and pain without judgment or criticism.

- I am able to transform my negative emotions into opportunities for growth and change.

Self-Esteem

- *I give myself permission to appreciate my worth and uniqueness.*

- *I am able to see the good in myself and others, even when things seem difficult.*

- *I welcome my flaws and imperfections, knowing they make me unique and special.*

- *I am able to express myself authentically and genuinely, without fear of judgment.*

- *I give myself permission to take control of my life and make positive choices for my well-being.*

Personal Transformation

- *I am able to change and grow at any point in my life.*

- *I give myself permission to explore new possibilities and experience life in different ways.*

- *I am able to embrace my uniqueness and appreciate my differences.*

- *I accept my mistakes as part of my growth and learning.*

- *I am able to find inner peace and happiness through the acceptance and integration of all parts of myself.*

Compassion and Kindness

- *I am kind and compassionate with myself, regardless of my imperfections.*

- *I give myself permission to take care of myself and dedicate the necessary time to my well-being.*

- *I am able to see the good in others and treat them with kindness and respect.*

- *I welcome my fragility and vulnerability without judgment or criticism.*

- *I give myself permission to be empathetic and help others when they need it.*

Gratitude

- *I am grateful for all the experiences that have brought me to this point in my life.*
- *I give myself permission to appreciate the small things in life and find beauty in the everyday.*
- *I am able to find gratitude even in difficult and painful situations.*
- *I welcome gratitude as part of my daily well-being practice.*
- *I am grateful for the loved ones in my life and their support and love.*

Mindfulness

- *I am present in the present moment and aware of my thoughts, emotions, and sensations.*
- *I give myself permission to slow down and enjoy the present without worries about the past or future.*
- *I am able to observe my thoughts and emotions without judgment or criticism.*
- *I welcome mindfulness as part of my daily well-being practice.*
- *I am able to find inner peace through the practice of mindfulness.*

Authenticity

- *I am authentic and true to myself and others.*
- *I give myself permission to express myself authentically, even when things seem difficult.*
- *I am able to embrace my authenticity and live according to my values and beliefs.*
- *I welcome authenticity as part of my identity and well-being.*
- *I am able to find happiness and satisfaction in life through authentic expression of myself.*

How to Use the Affirmations

To get the most out of these affirmations, try reciting them daily, both in the morning and at night. You can also write them in a journal or repeat them mentally throughout theday. When reciting these affirmations, try to embody the feelings and emotions behind them, and visualize yourself fully embracing all parts of yourself.

Additionally, it can be helpful to reflect on any resistance or discomfort that arises while reciting these affirmations. This resistance may be an indication of areas where you need to focus on healing and integrating your shadow aspects.

Remember that this is a journey, and it may take time and effort to fully integrate all parts of yourself. But with patience, self-compassion, and consistent practice, you can cultivate a more loving and accepting relationship with yourself, and experience greater peace and fulfillment in your life.

THE SHADOW WORK JOURNAL

A Journey in Your Mind to Discover
Yourself and Embrace the Shadow

CONTENTS

PREFACE

Many people who are struggling with mental disorders may be reading this book. These struggles are very normal and are widely experienced. This book is meant to help people with all kinds of issues and struggles, but it is not a comprehensive treatment for mental disorders. The information herein cannot replace mental health treatment if you need it. If you have a serious condition of mental health condition, you should still try to seek help from a mental health professional because no single book can cure mental disorders.

If you only experience general unease or less serious issues, this book can be enough to help you, but if you have more ongoing and deeper issues, this book can be used in conjunction with therapeutic practices, and it is inspired by many therapeutic modalities. A book can never understand an individual's unique experiences, just as a mental health clinician cannot make blanket statements without knowing a person's unique needs and issues. Thus, it's important to take care of your mental health in any way necessary and to seek any help that you may need as part of this growth process.

If at any time, your feelings become too intense or confusing, please consult with a mental health professional who can help you process the feelings you are dealing with. Especially among people who have serious traumas, shadow work can be overwhelming if you don't have an adequate support system.

This Shadow Journal Belongs to:

Fill in with your name empty slots below and carefully read the following statements.

I _____ pledge to read this Shadow Journal from cover to cover which I understand to include all the contents it holds. I agree to read every word and to use the information given for my self-reflection to achieve self-awareness. Well using the contents of this journal, I fully intend to do my best to learn about my inner child with the intent to help me change any undesirable habits. I sign this with the full understanding that these exercises are intended to help me analyze both my subconscious and conscious so that I may perform these exercises in an effort to change unwanted habits.

I _____ pledge to perform all the useful exercises consistently to ensure the most desirable outcome for myself. With this pledge, I know that the level of effort I put in is directly linked to the outcome and success of changing my habits. I also acknowledge, I dedicate to these Shadow Journal exercises and I willingly undertake this endeavor with an open mind. I dedicate to exploring the authentic self within my subconscious and desire the healing of my inner child. I sign this with the intent to remove my anxiety and negativity to the best of my abilities and fully intend to complete this Shadow Journal.

Date: _____

Sign Here: _____

INTRODUCTION OF THE SHADOW WORK

There are parts of us all that we don't let other people fully know. We hide these parts of ourselves because we would rather not think of them. Do you feel like there's a dark, shadowy part of yourself holding you back from reaching your full potential and engaging fully in life? If you do, you're in good company. We all have dark parts of ourselves that can overtake the brightness and joy in our lives. Fortunately, by making peace with our shadow selves, we can illuminate how our past hurts have made us who we are and still impact our decisions today. We can then work to transform our thought processes to match our desires.

Around the world, there are millions of sufferers of stress and mental health disorders. Johns Hopkins suggests that in the United States, 26% of adults have some type of mental health condition, which doesn't include the general distress that every person goes through at some point in their lives. Of U.S. Adults, FHE states that 51% of women and 61% of men have experienced at least one traumatic moment in their life, and this highlights how prevalent trauma is among the general population. Trauma can be caused by various factors, and while some people are more prone to specific mental health conditions triggered by trauma, everyone has to deal with pain and negative feelings in their lives. These feelings can become overwhelming and make you feel like you cannot do the usual activities you love to do with the same enthusiasm and connection. Fortunately, this book answers the distress and hardships in your life by giving you tools and guidance to feel healthier and happier.

Your mindset is firmly attached to your health. While studies related to this connection are relatively young, the studies that have been completed show dramatic results, and they suggest that an insular focus on physical health isn't good enough to promote healthy (or happy) lives. The American Psychological Association endorses the value of the mind-body connection, which is the link between your physical state and your mental state. The World Health Organization includes mental health as part of its view of holistic health. Shadow work tackles this part of you by unpacking your unconscious thoughts and the role trauma has played in your life. It allows you to utilize the power of your brain and the way thinking in new ways can change your life.

Your shadow self may loom over you, but being aware of your mind-body connection, you can explore new areas of yourself. Think about how you feel when you are mentally or physically exhausted. If you've gone for a long run, it probably will be more exhausting to sit down and complete complicated math problems. Whether you have physical or mental exhaustion, you're not going to want to do other things, and it will be harder to find the energy to do so. However, you don't just have to trust anecdotal evidence.

The research showing the importance of your mind-body connection is profound, and it highlights that there's still a lot about the human mind that we must explore. Studies have shown how trauma doesn't just impact someone's emotional state, but also the structures of your brain, which have a role in everything you do. Heart disease, diabetes, cancer, and many other physical conditions become more prevalent when someone is mentally ill. Likewise, chronic conditions can result in mental disorders because of the strain they cause. Thus, people who have better mental health and a positive state of mind tend to live longer.

A research completed in Wales at Bangor University has put this mind-body connection under test by having people practice both a mentally challenging task and then a physically challenging task. The researchers then had requested participants to complete the same physically draining task when they were mentally rested, and of course, in the second scenario, participants were able to push through physically for longer. This research highlights how the way you feel, and the unconscious thoughts you have, do impact the way your body functions and how you can complete tasks. Even if you aren't aware of how your mind is impacting your overall well-being, your mental health is still doing so.

If you've had any trauma or suffering, especially in your childhood, this book can help you process your emotions through shadow work. When you haven't addressed your trauma, you become stuck. You do the same things and get frustrated when you still repeat them. You live life in one big circle, wanting desperately to do new things, but your trauma holds you back from making enriching changes and allowing yourself to become a dynamic human being. Being stagnant won't give you a rewarding relationship with the world or yourself. Thus, while it is hard to move forward, you need to do so to feel good about yourself.

Completing inner work is one of the best choices you can make for yourself. Inner work is about deeper issues within yourself that you can then apply to the bigger world. You can accomplish your goals by starting from within and letting your inner work influence your outer world. Those who are more self-aware tend to do better in their pursuits, and they can more easily define what they want. Additionally, they can deal with the challenges of life without feeling like they are losing themselves or that they don't know how to walk the path of their own lives. Life is scary and unpredictable, but inner work helps you learn to control what is in your power rather than worry about what is not.

You will discover the secrets of your shadow self and learn how it will improve your life. Right now, you might not realize how much you don't know about yourself! The beliefs you have about your own identity may be starkly different from the way other people see you. Learning more about yourself, therefore, is one of the most powerful things to change your life and learn to make peace with the dark parts of your life. If you've lost track of what you want, how you feel, or who you are, this book can help you get back on track and learn to emerge from the hold of your past and the way your brain is wired.

This book will help you define the changes you need to make. It's hard to know how to begin the process of improving yourself, so many people don't do it at all. They say, "I'll just stay where I am because it's better than having to figure out where I have to go." Think about planning a trip. When you are planning a vacation, it can be overwhelming when there are so many places to go and things to do. You need to define what you want before you decide where to go. Do you want to see the ocean? Are you dreaming of a cool ski trip? Each trip has very different qualities, so deciding what you want to do on any journey has to be one of the first steps you take.

Journaling is the main feature of this book. At the end of this book, you will have a journal that can guide you through your journey and help you to instill habits that will help you create ongoing change in your life. This journal will give you all the prompts you need to think about yourself in new ways and start self-exploration. This journal is something that will help you track your progress and see how far you have gone. By committing, you can start to rewire your unconscious brain and find harmony with the darker parts of yourself.

This journey won't always be easy. You'll have hard days, and there will be moments when you think you are failing, but the good news is that when you keep trying and stay committed to the process, you can see results. Even when you feel powerless in life, you always have the power to dictate the terms of your own self. For those of you who have been through traumatic events, you know that life often throws you obstacles that you feel ill equipped to handle, but shadow work helps you take away the mystique and fear of those events. Trauma doesn't have to shape you.

It takes time and effort to complete this book, but by completing it, you set yourself up for success. No matter what you'd like to do in your life, shadow work can help. No person has had a perfect life, and no person can erase their shadow selves, but that doesn't mean you have to let your shadow self control you. It's time to begin your healing journey and live a fuller life.

THE BEGINNING OF YOUR SHADOW WORK JOURNAL

"It is only through shadows that one comes to know the light."

— St. Catherine of Siena —

THE IMPACT OF SHADOW WORK

Shadow work is a tool you can use to confront painful and embarrassing parts of yourself that make you want to hide rather than be fully alive and engaged with the world around you. As you start to do this shadow work, you'll feel positive changes within yourself, but first, you have to understand the nature of shadow work and why it is so impactful.

What Is Shadow Work?

Shadow work is all about the unconscious mind, and it generally represents the dark parts of yourself that we hide, but that darkness doesn't always relate to the bad parts of you. Though, when parts of you are in the shadow, you can experience a disconnection from yourself and be unable to live genuinely. Shadow work is the idea that for you to grow and develop as a person, you need to confront the dark parts of yourself that you have repressed and live in your unconscious mind. Your shadow sits opposite of your ego, and these two forces cannot exist without each other, so finding harmony between these forces allows growth.

Carl Jung, a Swiss psychiatrist, is the father of shadow work. He once answered the question about how to find your shadow by saying, "How do you find a dragon that has swallowed you?" Jung studied personality and how a shadow can make certain hurts and dark parts of yourself repressed. This repression causes a lot of pain, and it impacts your behaviors. Each person is born with their whole self, but because of the way the world operates, we have to deny certain parts of ourselves to fit in and even survive. Our whole self is split between our ego and our shadow.

Your unconscious mind is powerful. People often underestimate the power of their unconscious minds because it's hard to quantify the power of these thoughts. Research published in Behavioral and Brain Sciences studied how much unconscious thoughts influence your behavior, and the results suggest that most thoughts are unconscious. Some research says that up to 95% of all brain activity is unconscious. Therefore, learning to influence t he unconscious brain can revolutionize the way you think, feel, and act.

Consider your habits. Your unconscious mind is all about your habits. The way you go to work, how you make your coffee, and the order you shampoo your hair and clean your body in the shower are all examples of habits. You do these things without thinking about them, and it saves you time. While deciding whether to shampoo first or wash your body doesn't seem like it would take a lot of energy to decide, if you had to make all those little decisions each day, it would add a lot of time and energy. Habits are shortcuts that help you behave more efficiently, and your brain likes habits because they

are easier, and because you have done them so many times before, they feel safe. However, habits don't always cause good: biting nails, drug abuse, overeating, and smoking are all examples of how habitual behavior can cause negative results. Only by becoming aware of your habits and adding new habits to get rid of old ones can you reorient yourself. These habits highlight the way your brain can act without you consciously realizing what it is doing. This is also true of your shadow self, but upon reflection, you can address your unconscious thoughts and make them conscious.

One study by Stefano et al. tried to determine if employees could improve their performance by reflecting up on th eir mistakes. The results of this study were astounding, and employees who took the time for reflection performed 23% better than employees who were not allowed to take reflection time. The even better news i s that these results started within a mere fifteen minutes. Thus, the changes you need to make to increase your performance and ability to succeed aren't that much of an investment. But more than just productivity, people who can engage in self-reflection are happier than those who can't. Shadow work is one of the best ways to self-reflect because it promotes self-honesty.

You can have an improved relationship with yourself when you take the time to understand yourself. Shadow work is all about integrating the parts of the shadow into your personality. It's about learning to accept even the parts of you that are wedged deep down.

DEEPER CONCEPTS OF SHADOW WORK

Shadow work is more than just dealing with your darker self. It is learning to illuminate that darkness and find more balance in your life. Furthermore, it incorporates many other concepts, and your shadow self is more complex than you may realize. Understanding some of the deeper concepts of shadow work can help you engage in this journal more completely. People can be conscious of their shadows, and the ego can control the shadow, but the goal of shadow work is to learn awareness so that the shadow cannot be autonomous.

Personal Shadow Versus Collective Shadow

Carl Jung defines people as having two classifications of shadows: the personal and the collective. While your shadow is the part of you that is unconsciously dark, the collective shadow is the darkness that is unconscious among the larger society. Understanding each of these shadows can help you find personal growth that extends beyond just yourself and is useful to the greater world around you.

"The thing a person has no wish to be," Jung explains to show what the personal shadow is. The personal shadow is unconscious, hidden parts of yourself that you don't even want to admit to yourself that you have, let alone admit as much to other people. These are qualities of the ego that make us feel inferior. These inferiorities are things we want to avoid. It makes sense that we wouldn't want to face parts of ourselves that we perceive as embarrassing, shameful, and lesser, but the issue is that things that are obscured are still there. The shadow still appears when we are struggling; it shows up when we are acting in self-destructive ways that don't match how we'd ideally like to behave.

The collective shadow represents the impact of the greater world on a person's shadow self. This collective shadow doesn't so much pertain the personal traumas, but it reflects societal values. It often focuses on the harm that humans cause to other people and the earth. It is the darkness that follows our collective identity as humans.

For example, think of oppressed people, war, climate change, and other similar darknesses we experience. These speak to the collective shadow and the ways it can cause pain and destruction in our lives. The collective shadow isn't always so obvious. For example, missionaries can bring darkness under the guise of doing good.

The collective and personal shadows interact with each other. For example, if someone is oppressed because of their religion, they may start to internalize the messages the oppressive society is telling them about themselves. Similarly, internalized racism can occur when the dominant culture creates harmful messaging about a certain race. For instance, western beauty standards often prioritize features that are more common among white people of European ancestry. Someone who does not fit those standards may want to emulate them and have internalized prejudices about their own race as a result. Dealing with these feelings can cause a lot of pain, and it also makes people feel disconnected from themselves and their culture.

For both types of shadows, the

most important step that people can take to control the bad impacts of personal or societal shadows is to confront those shadows by bringing them out of the darkness and shining a light on their true nature. People need to be aware of why they are acting the way they are, and shadow work allows them to do that with precision. The shadow doesn't go away until you learn to make it conscious and begin to unpack all that it represents and stands for. People often want to deny bad things, but denial only drives you away from integrating the shadows of yourself and the world.

What Happens When You Ignore Your Shadow?

Ignoring your shadow, as you can likely guess, causes a lot of negative consequences. Your whole demeanor can change when your shadow is allowed to do as it pleases without any control. You could be extremely moody and quick to anger. You may snap at family or coworkers because the dark forces within you are causing chaos. These feelings are especially hard because you often don't know why they are happening. The shadow self is mostly unconscious; therefore, you have negative feelings that seem to come from nowhere, when really they are all about the shadow.

There are good qualities inherent in your shadow self. These qualities show your potential and strength, but when you ignore these qualities, you lose that potential, and you miss out on chances for enrichment. Your unconscious brain starts to work against you, and you become a self-fulfilling prophecy, embodying the traits you don't like and being unwittingly consumed by the darkness of your shadow self. For example, you may think that asserting yourself is aggression, and as a result, you may allow other people to disrespect you, and you may miss chances for growth opportunities like career advancement. You become stuck despite wanting to do better. You then become resentful of people who are advancing, which makes the shadow self angrier, and that anger of only does more damage.

If you ignore your shadow self, you lose some degree of control over your mental state. Your trauma and hurt rear their heads without warning, and as a result, you can damage your relationships, career, and personal endeavors. People who ignore their shadow selves are commonly enacting self-sabotage, meaning they act in ways that hurt their ability to do the things they most want to do. This self-sabotage is usually protective because changes are threatening to the shadow self, and it feels safer to keep yourself where you are and avoid the risk of doing things that could psychologically backfire.

Your Shadow Gives Potential

Your shadow self isn't a terrible beast. It represents what you can be in life. By using your shadow to your advantage, you can complete any goals you have. You can lessen the impact of your negative traits and emphasize the positive traits that make you your truest self. The more you listen to the shadow and do this shadow work, the more potential you will unlock.

The Shadow is Not Just Evil

Each negative factor in your life has a positive intent that you can heal and reframe so that you can overcome the negativity in your life. Many scholars suggest that the shadow isn't necessarily just the dark parts of your personality. It represents the things we lack, and with the shadow, our personality can be whole. For example, a timid person may have an assertive shadow self. Assertiveness can be a positive trait, but when it is part of the shadow self, it can lead to projection and bitterness when people see it in others. In general, the shadow self represents the good, the bad, and the in-between that exists within all of us.

Jung uses the idea of the shadow self and its terrible tendencies in *Archetypes and the Collec ive Unconscious*. Carl Jung says the shadow self "displays a number of good qualities, such as normal instincts, appropriate reactions, realistic insights, creative impulses, etc.". The shadow self is more than just all the bad parts of yourself, because when you learn to listen to it and tend to it, you find parts of yourself that allow you to behave and react to the world in more appropriate manners, and you learn to open your mind rather than limiting it.

Jungian scholars have furthered this idea in their own works. For example, Marie-Louise von Franz posits that the shadow doesn't have to be your enemy; rather, the relationships we have with our shadow selves are very much like the relationships we have with other people. Sometimes, we learn to get along with others by giving in. Other times, we resist or offer the person love. We base these decisions on how to deal with other people on what's needed in that specific situation. Thus, the same is true of the shadow self. We react to our shadows based on what they need, and it is not always an adversarial relationship.

When you misunderstand and ignore your shadow, it becomes adversarial. Consider your relationships that have had issues. Often, it is a misunderstanding that causes a relationship to become adversarial. When you don't see eye to eye on something and cannot understand one another's point of view, it becomes hard to give love or respect.

Your shadow is the force that carries your inner child, the little version of you that has been hurt and continues to be hurt. Children don't want to fight. They want to be nurtured and paid attention to, and your shadow self demands that same kind of treatment.

The Shadow Is More Than It Seems

Shadow work strives to look at the complexity of humans rather than simplifying us to be just one thing or the other. Many people think that the shadow is something they should avoid when that couldn't be further from the truth. In fact, that kind of avoidance does more harm than good. Several parts make up the shadow. It is never just one part of yourself, so it cannot be reduced to represent just evil or just potential. It is not just darkness or light. Without light, a shadow cannot exist, just as it cannot exist if there is only light. While the shadow may seem like it's a distinct, negative force that lives within you, it is fully part of you. Thus, learning to love our shadow selves is better than learning to hate those parts of us.

Your Shadow Causes Projection

Projection is a psychological term that refers to when you take a quality you don't like about yourself and put it on others. If you don't like a certain part of yourself, you are more likely to see that trait in other people and become highly reactive. This reaction is more about yourself than it is about the other person. You are hateful of your own traits, but you cannot make peace with those feelings, so you project those negative feelings onto other people.

Not only is a projection not liking similar traits to yours when they are in other people, but it can cause you to see similarities even in places where they may not exist. For example, if a man is cheating on his wife with another woman, that man may see his wife with other men and think that *she's* cheating, even when he has no solid reaons to think that is the case. Likewise, a person may dislike a coworker, but instead of confronting these feelings, they start to think their coworker doesn't like them despite that coworker always being friendly. The coworker's friend-liness can even cause an angry reaction because of the tendency of projection.

Others Impact Your Shadow

You are not an isolated being, which means that your social connections and role in the world all influence your shadow self. Much of your shadow self stems from forces outside of you. When others hurt you, their reactions and behaviors may cause you to hide certain parts of yourself and repress those parts because they are hard to face. Interestingly, because we often don't know our own shadows, it is often other people who see our shadow self first. People are collective beings, meaning that society and our relationships with other people greatly affect our shadow selves and the work we need to do to address those shadow selves.

WHAT SHADOW WORK ACCOMPLISHES

Shadow work allows you to be happier, but how does it accomplish that? Well, there are several ways that shadow works can promote more balance in your life, which Jungian practitioners have uncovered and continue to explore to better understand the nature of the human mind.

Assimilating Your Shadow Self

While it may be tempting to continue your current path and keep on projecting and denying your shadow self, shadow work allows you to assimilate your shadow self with your genuine self. Shadow work asks you to assimilate your ego and your shadow self so that your personality can work as a whole. There's always a part of us that is going to be in the shadow, but we want to make as much of our shadow selves conscious as we can, which can be a lifelong process, but it gets much easier as we practice healthy techniques.

One Jungian author, Robert A. Johnson, had many psychological troubles, starting after a near death experience when he was young. He wrote about the ways Carl Jung influenced him. Jung told him to do inner work, and eventually, Johnson wrote the book *Owning Your Own Shadow* to showcase how people can explore their inner worlds. Johnson points out that people don't just hide their dark parts, but even more fastidiously, they hide the noble aspects of their shadow. He continues to say, "To draw the skeleton out of the closet is easy, but to own the gold in the shadow is terrifying." He speaks of being vulnerable, which is one of the biggest challenges of shadow work, but it is through being vulnerable that we learn to assimilate and act in ways that make us feel content and enriched.

In this process, we must remember that we cannot get rid of our qualities, but we can nurture them in ways that bring out the good sides or the bad sides of those qualities. It is finding a balance between the different parts of ourselves that allows us to be in equilibrium. Think of it like carrying a long rod with buckets of water on either end. You are trying to walk with the buckets, and imagine that on one side, there are four buckets while on the other side, there is just one. The imbalance makes it harder to walk with the buckets. This imbalance can cause moodiness and general discontent. When you even the load on each side, you can continue your process more easily. Thus, you must assimilate your shadow self.

Part of assimilation is bringing the shadow back to where it came from. Because of projection, the collective shadow, and the way people's shadows can confront one another, the shadow can wander so far from where it initially was, and for assimilation to take place, you must bring it back into yourself and focus on internal wholeness. When we can bring our ego and shadow back together, we can find love, the synthesis of all the good and bad parts of ourselves; in love, we find care and compassion even in imperfection. We find acceptance from others and ourselves. We become energized when we finally confront our shadows.

Authenticity

When you do shadow work, you can be more authentic. Exploring your shadow self gives you the truth, and when you have this truth, it will feel like a weight is taken off your shoulders because you can be your authentic self. You can stop wanting to hide the parts of you that are dark and learn to embrace them. You begin to overcome the shame and self hate that hold you back. Authenticity is all about discovering the deepest parts of yourself. This process can be long, but when you commit to it, you rediscover who you are, and you feel like a unified person rather than a bunch of mismatched parts.

Finding the Good in Yourself

Jung emphasizes that dealing with the shadow self helps you not only understand the bad deeds you are capable of, but it helps you know the good deeds you are capable of. Your shadow, when it is unaddressed, makes you feel like you exist in the darkness. There is always good in you, just as there is always bad in you. There's nothing wrong with having both forces; it is human, but you want to try to focus on the forces that promote.

Self-Confidence

It's hard to feel confident when there's a whole part of yourself that you are ignoring. Your shadow self, when it remains unknown, may try to tear you down. It may fuel negative thoughts. Some common negative thoughts people have include:

- I am not good enough
- I am dumb and stupid
- I will never accomplish my goals
- I am a broken person, and I can't be fixed
- I am lazy
- I'm a terrible employee
- I'm rude and mean
- I'll never be a good spouse or parent
- My life is crumbling around me
- People are going to see that I am not competent

There are so many negative beliefs that we automatically assume are true, and these thoughts often stem from our pasts and how those pasts have shaped our perception of the world. By starting to unpack these thoughts, you can find freedom from your self-doubt.

Improved Relationships

If you are having a lot of relationship problems, there's a good chance that you may be struggling with your shadow self. Past relationships often shape how you behave in new relationships, but confronting your shadow self can help you improve the thoughts you have related to relationships. You can get closer to others by knowing yourself better. Because you cannot fully express yourself if you hide parts of who you are, it's going to be hard to share parts of yourself with others. Additionally, when your shadow self is unaddressed, you may be moodier, and your overflowing emotions could result in your relationships starting to deteriorate. Relationships require vulnerability, and you can create deeper connections with people by being more vulnerable.

Inner Peace

When you do the shadow work, you will feel calmer. All the noise in your brain will become manageable, and you'll learn to have compassion for yourself and accept all your traits. You don't need to love all traits equally, but you will learn to embrace them. You will then be able to extend compassion to other people in your life, creating a cycle of giving good and getting it back.

WHAT MAKES SHADOW WORK HARD?

For all the good things that shadow work can do for you, there are also many things it does that can cause you to struggle. You might wonder if shadow work is the right path for you.

Understanding the challenges you will face before you start delving in can help you know that some struggle is normal and that you need to keep going.

Taking Time to Discover Yourself

There are only so many hours in the day, and when you are starting shadow work, you may be dismayed by the fact that you have to set aside time to do this work. Most people have busy lives. They have careers and families, and chances are that they are overwhelmed by trying to balance all of this. However, if you choose to make something a priority, you can find the time you need. Watching just a little less TV, for example, can give you enough time to do this shadow work. Additionally, once you have done the work, you will free up quality time to be more efficient and be more present when you are spending time with others.

Honesty Isn't Easy

The truth is not always the easiest option. Each person on this earth has lied, and often, the person we lie the most to is ourselves. Some truths are nearly unthinkable and reflecting upon them can bring up difficult memories. The truth takes courage, and shadow work will require

you to find that courage. You don't have to be honest about everything all at once, but you do have to accept that you can't keep obscuring the truth if you want to improve your life.

If the honesty gets to be too much, seek the help of a professional who can help you better understand what is going on with you and safely process the emotions or memories that you are experiencing. It can also help to talk to a friend about your shadow work process, so you know you have someone to turn to if you have struggles going forward.

Uncovering What Is Hidden

When things are hidden, they are often covered in layers that protect them from being seen. Think of the biggest secret you have, or if you cannot initially think of one, think of a big secret someone you know or a character in a story had. All these stories likely have a similarity of people working hard to make sure that the secret doesn't come out. Some of you might have even tried to immediately push one of your secrets from the forefront of your mind because you don't even want to think about it! Things that are hidden are often wrapped in lies and feelings related to that secret, and you have to do a lot of unwrapping and uncovering before you can even access those hidden things. Therefore, shadow work can be draining and feel impossible.

Finding Joy in Hardship

When a journey is hard, it might be challenging to find joy on that journey, but it's important that you try to look on the bright side. Your negativity will make you want to retreat and look away from your shadow self. While you may remember painful memories or feelings, that doesn't mean that you won't also uncover joyous things. For example, think of a child whose parent died when they were young, and they buried some of those feelings related to their parent's death. With those painful memories of loss, the child might have also buried happy memories with their parent. The shadow self doesn't just hold onto the loss, but it holds onto and controls the things you have gained and the things you can be grateful to have.

You Cannot Control What You Discover

No matter how careful you are, you cannot control the parts of yourself that you may discover, which is incredibly terrifying for many people starting shadow work. You may learn things about yourself that you couldn't have anticipated and that you would get rid of in an instant if it were up to you. Unfortunately, part of the process is learning that you cannot change what you find within yourself. Don't worry; as you go on this journey, you'll realize that there's more of yourself to love than to hate.

Don't Expect Perfection

You cannot expect to become the perfect person because of shadow work. In his work, *Psychology and Alchemy*, Carl Jung says, "There is no light without shadow and no psychic wholeness without imperfection." Shadow work is all about finding balance within yourself. You will always have a distinction between conscious and unconscious thoughts, but it is learning to help those realms exist together that makes shadow work so life changing. You want to align your shadow self with your genuine self. The shadow may seem dark and scary, but there is room for that shadow in you because that shadow is you, even if just a part. The ultimate goal is to be a complete and balanced person.

START GETTING TO KNOW YOUR SHADOW

"One does not become enlightened by imagining figures of light, but by making the darkness conscious."

- Carl Jung -

THE BEGINNING OF THE SHADOW WORK JOURNEY

This journal was created for those ready to confront their dark side and discover the shadow within them. The path of shadow work is an intense and profound journey that requires dedication and perseverance, but the results will be incredible.

Remember that the path of shadow work can be difficult but extremely rewarding. By facing your dark sides and integrating them into your life, you can become more authentic, compassionate, and self-aware regarding yourself and others. You are encouraged to start this journey, accept the challenges you will encounter along the way, and take care of yourself during the transformation process.

Meeting Yourself

As you get started on this journey, you will want to get to know yourself better through your shadow. Before you can even reach the shadow, you have to think about the perception you already have of yourself. Your shadow speaks to many of the parts of yourself you keep hidden. Many people become disconnected from their own emotions and lose a sense of self in the process. Thus, you may feel like you are meeting yourself as if you are a new person because of that disconnect. There are many things that you may have forgotten about yourself because of trauma or hardships, which this book will help you unpack in various days of journaling. Today is all about remembering who you are, what you stand for, and what work you need to do going forward. Today you will get in touch with what gives you energy in life and how you identify. This is the foundation you will use for your ongoing work.

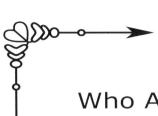
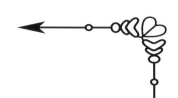

Who Am I?

My name is _____. I am _____ years old, and my occupation is _____. In my spare time, I love to _____, _____, _____. These are just a few important elements of my life.

Three words I use to describe myself are_____, _____, and _____.

I love that I can

_____
_____
_____
_____
_____

I define myself as

_____
_____
_____
_____
_____

My biggest dream is to

_____
_____
_____
_____
_____

Some of the most important people in my life are

_____
_____
_____
_____
_____

I want my future to be _____, _____,
_____,_____, _____, and
_____

From this Shadow path, I expect that

_____
_____
_____
_____
_____

I feel that Shadow Work can help me for

_____
_____
_____
_____
_____

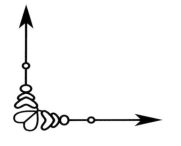
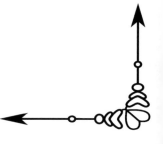

Meeting the Shadow

While meeting your shadow and meeting yourself may seem to be the same task, the focus of today is on the shadow elements of yourself and how they relate to your full self. The goal is to reflect on the things you keep hidden and how they influence your behaviors, thoughts, feelings, and how you interact with the world. Starting to meet the shadow means accepting that you will encounter parts of yourself on this journey that you might not know how to handle.

You aren't going to have a strong relationship with your shadow quite yet because it takes weeks to gain traction on your shadow work; however, you can start to introduce yourself to your shadow self right now.

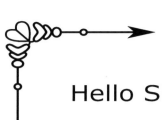
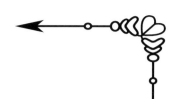

Hello Shadow

Draw a picture of your shadow. Don't overthink what your shadow looks like. Draw this portrait based on your instinctual, imaginative idea of what your shadow looks like. Your shadow doesn't have to be human like, either!

What You Lock Away

Write several sentences about the things you hide within yourself. Imagine that you have a box in your gut that you fill with a bunch of stuff. What parts of you do you put in that box? What does that stuff look like?

_____

_____

_____

_____

_____

_____

_____

_____

_____

_____

_____

_____

_____

_____

_____

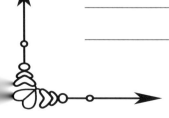

Making Space for Joy

The goal of life is to be happy. Happiness doesn't mean that nothing bad happens to you or that you are always in the best mood. However, it does mean that you have an overall sense of content, and even in hard times, you can go back to a baseline state of happiness. This baseline state of happiness allows you to resist negative forces, be healthier, and in general, feel better about yourself.

While it is one of the most important parts of life, joy is something that many people are missing because they don't know how to find space in their lives for it. When you have a busy life, you may be rushing through your daily activities, and in the process, you become disconnected. You get so caught up in getting things done and fulfilling your duties that you don't enjoy the normal parts of your life.

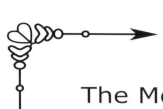
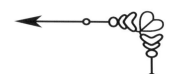

The Most Joyous Things

Circle the five things on this list that give you the most joy from the following list:

Family	**Building**
Work	**Love**
Home	**Movies**
Friends	**Treats**
School	**Books**
Games	**Physical Activity**
Hobbies	**Beverages**
Travel	**Crafts**
Music	**Time Away**
Food	**Tea or Coffee**
Television	**Pets**
Nature	**Sleep**
Art	**Dance**
Vacations	

Where Joy Lives

Imagine you have a big building, and you can fill it with whatever things you want. What would this building look like? What
would it have? How would you engage with this building?

_____

_____

_____

_____

_____

_____

_____

_____

_____

_____

_____

_____

_____

The Clutter in Your Mind

Think about when your house is a mess. Your stuff is thrown all around the floor, stacked up in haphazard piles. To find anything, you need to dig through all the piles until you find what you need. In the process, you end up making more of a mess, and the more mess you have, the harder it becomes to declutter because you don't even know where to start! The same is true of your mind. Like your house, your brain can easily get cluttered with a lot of negative and warped thoughts. These thoughts can confuse you and make it hard to be your fullest self.

Today, you will start a process of spring cleaning by beginning to differentiate clutter from meaningful thoughts and beliefs you have. Generally speaking, you can identify clutter by finding what parts of your life make you feel stressed or anxious.

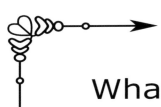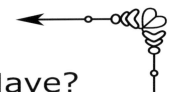

What Clutter Do You Have?

Take a few minutes to write about the clutter in your life that makes it hard for you to function as well as you would like.

_____

_____

_____

_____

_____

_____

_____

_____

_____

_____

_____

_____

_____

Declutter Checklist

Write a checklist with ten things that clutter your mind. You can then take steps to replace these things with more positive forces.

1. _____

2. _____

3. _____

4. _____

5. _____

6. _____

7. _____

8. _____

9. _____

10. _____

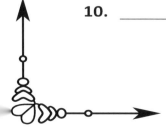
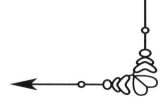

Being Grateful

To bring your shadow self to the surface and face the darkness in your life, you also have to acknowledge the light. Yes, there will be plenty of obstacles that you won't like. Each day, you will face challenges that you'd rather not have; however, focusing on all that's going wrong in your life doesn't make all the good things a priority. When you can appreciate the positive parts of life, you can focus on things that are within your control and make useful changes.

Gratitude is about acknowledging the positives in your life, even in negative experiences, no matter how big or small. This process is harder when your shadow has overtaken your life and has made you believe that there is no good. When you assume that everything will go wrong, it will go wrong, so it's time to confront those doubts and start to find silver linings in everything you do.

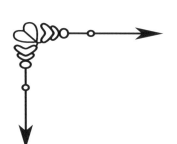
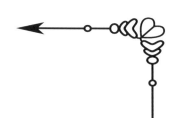

Gratitude List

List fifteen things you are grateful for.

1. _____

2. _____

3. _____

4. _____

5. _____

6. _____

7. _____

8. _____

9. _____

10. _____

11. _____

12. _____

13. _____

14. _____

15. _____

GO INTO THE SHADOW WORK JOURNAL

"Shadow-making happens in families and makes us who we are. It leads to shadow-work, which makes us who we can become."

— CONNIE ZWEIG -

ANALYSIS OF SELF

A crucial part of shadow work is learning to analyze yourself. This process can be intimidating and draining, but it doesn't have to be that hard. It will require work, but when you take a holistic approach to self-analysis, you can make sure you don't get overwhelmed.

What Is Self-Analysis?

Self-analysis, also known as self-assessment, means that you study key parts of your identity to create self-knowledge and self-confidence. *The Analysis of the Self* was a work written by Heinz Kohut, a psychoanalyst. While the work focuses on narcissism, one of its key takeaways is the idea that the human self is created based on the relationships we have and how we relate to others. Self-harmony does not disconnect us from other people, but it unifies us with them.

This unity doesn't mean that a person is not autonomous, but it means that they understand their greater human connection.

Since Kohut's writings, the understanding of the self has evolved, and many other modalities tackle handling the self and integrating one's identity with their genuine self. These modalities have a place in self-growth because while the true nature of the human mind holds many mysteries, psychological theories help us better understand how we can rewire our brains to have happier and healthier lives.

When certain things are repressed, children may grow up unable to have a healthy self-esteem and a sense of self. Trauma can disconnect people from themselves and the necessary engagement with the world around them. Self-analysis allows people to deal with messages and beliefs that they have internalized and that are holding them back from creating growth. Self-analysis is a vital part of shadow work because it shows the work you have to do to take on your unconscious thoughts and bring them to the surface so that you can create better habits.

Why Is Self-Analysis Important?

Self-analysis helps you motivate yourself because it allows you to have momentum with whatever endeavors you want to complete. It allows you to unpack the mistakes you have made and reflect on all the things you have done right. As a result, you can make decisions going forward that are productive rather than self-destructive. Without self-analysis, you can become complacent, and you start to think that there's no point in trying to do anything else because you don't believe the changes you want can happen. Self-analysis ensures you don't get stuck in bad habits that cannot possibly bring you increased well-being.

When you can analyze yourself, you can highlight your strengths. We all have things that make us better, and these are what we need to channel when we are trying to make progress. It may be hard to embrace the fullness of our skills if we are held back by our shadow selves.

You need to discover what limits you have. Understanding your limits helps you know when to push those limits and when to resist. For example, someone who is impulsive can get into habits that limit their impulses. They could get in the habit of stopping before making decisions and forcing themselves to go through a mental checklist. For every trait or limit that causes you to struggle, there are options to reduce the negative impact of that struggle. All you have to do is be aware of what holds you back.

How to Analyze Yourself

Get in touch with your senses. Pay attention to how you see yourself. How does your physical self represent your emotional self? Remember that your senses are more than just your eyes. If you struggle to connect to your other senses, try closing your eyes and paying more attention to the senses of taste, touch, smell, and hearing. You can access your emotional cues by noticing your senses. Your body will often react to certain stimuli in the same way. Never forget that the link between your body and your mind is so powerful and can illuminate what you are feeling.

Listen to your emotions, even if you'd rather ignore them. Your emotions contain many highs and lows, but they are auseful feedback that can help you step forward. Every time you have an emotion, it means something. It may be hard to understand the meanings of those emotions. At first, you may be so disconnected that it's hard to identify them, but as you get into the practice of paying attention to your emotions, you'll be better at understanding them.

Explore parts of yourself that make you feel shame. When you start to feel little sensations of shame, don't try to rush those sensations out of your body. Dig deeper. Sometimes, you must put pressure on a wound to get

it to stop bleeding and start the healing process. That's what you have to do in your process of self-analysis.

Shame is something most people have, and while it feels terrible, it can give a lot of good feedback about how you feel, what you want, and who you are.

Find a higher power. It can be God or any other deity that you worship, but it doesn't have to be anything religious. Your higher power reminds you that there's more to the world than just yourself. Some forces are much greater than you, and you are part of those forces. Mother Nature can be a higher power; friendship could also be a higher power. You will interact with your higher power in a way that's unique to you and reflects your personality and view of the world. Your higher power helps ground you and understand yourself better.

Learn about yourself through connection. Connecting to other people also helps you learn more about yourself. Talk to people about the things you discover about yourself, and while you don't want to rely solely on the opinions of others, understanding the way other people see you can help you learn new things about yourself. Don't automatically assume that the perceptions of others represent your true self, but use the information to promote further analysis.

What to Watch for During Self-Analysis

When you are analyzing yourself, you want to observe several things and watch out for certain patterns. When you look out for these things, you can start to notice your behavioral trends and any thought patterns that may be shaping your decisions.

Notice the trends in how you feel. This doesn't just mean when you are actively trying to complete self-analysis. You should also pay attention to how you are feeling in general to promote a more open internal dialogue. Some people struggle to acknowledge their feelings, and men can be especially at risk for being out of touch with their feelings because of societal ex-

pectations that men should be strong and not show weakness. Don't be afraid to show that you are feeling a certain way. Feelings themselves are not dangerous; it is actions that can become dangerous. Thus, allowing your feelings to exist is never a bad thing.

Instead of being judgmental, be curious. Don't think, "Oh, this thing about me makes me a bad person." The things you discover about yourself don't necessarily define your moral value. Bad qualities or dark traits don't make you a bad person. Just as good traits alone can't make you a good person. Each thing you learn is a chance to learn more, so don't shut down the learning experience by letting judgment taint your perception.

Take breaks when you need them. Throughout the process of self-analysis, you may get overwhelmed by some of the feelings you have. If things get to be too much, step away for a few moments and do whatever you need to do to collect yourself.

HOW TO USE THIS BOOK

There's no single "right" way to use it, and this book has left a lot of room for you to use it in the way that you see fit, but there are certain steps you should take if you want to maximize the potential of this book and use it as fully as you can.

Get Your Journal

Keeping a journal is vital in this process. Fortunately, this book has many journal prompts and content that can help you ask the right questions and begin to understand and communicate with your shadow self.

Research shows that journaling regularly for at least fifteen minutes each day can make you happier and reduce your stress. But that's not all! People who journal tend to be physically healthier, and journaling boosts your immune system so that you can resist illnesses. If that isn't enough to make you want to start journaling right now, journaling is a great opportunity to allow you to learn about yourself and what you want. Often, people get detached from their feelings, and journaling is one of the best grounding forces. Journaling won't solve all your problems, but it will give you a great starting point for making the necessary changes to reduce your hardships.

Feel free to journal beyond the parameters of this book. It will give very specific prompts that you can follow to discover your shadow self, but if you want to explore other areas of your life, your journal can help you there as well. When you have thoughts that you don't know how to process, journaling can help. It is also a fantastic way to discuss frustrations or concerns you may have along the way. Journaling can be what-ever you need it to be, so feel free to expand upon how this book suggests you journal.

Be creative in the process of using your journal to the fullest. Your imagination is your friend when you're journaling. The prompts don't have to be taken in literal terms. If another interpretation of the prompt speaks to you, go ahead and see what that route reaps. Additionally, you can customize the way you answer these prompts to reflect your unique circumstances.

If the prompts open new ideas, let those thoughts flow freely. When you've got your creative juices flowing, ideas that you don't expect may awaken. You don't have to change what you're writing about when you get off the prompt. Sometimes, writing freely can give you the most progress. The prompts are just a starting point, and as you continue to follow them, they can help your unconscious mind communicate with you. When you are in the zone of writing, it's nice to see where those thoughts take you.

Journaling is all about getting in touch with yourself and making revelations about your shadow self, so remember that you can customize it in any way you want. Remember to make sure you aren't journaling to avoid your shadow self.

Keep an Open Mind

If you don't believe something will work, there's no way that it can work. So many people harden their hearts, and they think, "No one can help me. Nothing can make me better." Or they think, "I shouldn't need help. This should be something I can do on my own." These thoughts aren't productive because they prevent you from opening your mind to opportunities. Pride can make you impede progress; resist that tendency.

Wondering if you're doing the right thing is normal. Doubts are often a product of your fear. They are normal and expected. Asking questions as you go is good. Questions can help you process the emotions you are feeling, and they are actually a great way to resist the doubts you have. When you keep an open mind, you invite new opportunities and the potential for positive change.

Have Clear Intentions

Before you start the journal prompts, you need to know what you want out of the experience. When you don't know what your intentions are, it's pretty intimidating to start your journey. Consider the most dominant problems. What are the major obstacles in your life that you want to correct? Think about what you want to do in the next few years. How are you going to magnify the joy you already have? Then, you can identify what your ultimate goal is for this process. When you have clear intentions, you can stay on track to reaching those goals and shape your shadow work to match what you want to accomplish.

Consistency Is Key

As with any journal, consistency is one of the most important parts of the process. Put in some effort every day. Make sure that you get in the habit of using the practices expressed in this book. While it's important to be consistent, you also have to know what you can do. Don't expect too much of yourself. Pushing yourself is good but overexerting yourself can make you so stressed that you don't want to continue with your shadow work anymore. When you get a consistent system, you are empowered to improve how you function.

Remind Yourself That Growth Takes Time

Unfortunately, growth doesn't happen instantly, so you must be patient with this process. Know that your shadow self is always part of you. You can't escape it, but you can learn to work with it. You should also set flexible goals, not deadlines. Don't push yourself faster than you need to. Growth is not linear. Your journey won't always feel good, but if you persevere whenever challenges stand in your path, you will get the result you need for growth. Patience is vital if you want to have a better connection to who you inherently are. Once you have patience, you will go far.

Carry On After This Book Is Done

This book is not supposed to just be something you hurry through and close forever. Keep working on the journal constantly every day and especially when you feel the need. As you continue, pay more attention to your shadow self. Your journal entries will be great for you to reflect upon going forward. They will help you see how you have developed. You can always go back to these entries to track your progress, and you can even reuse the prompts to see how your mindset is different now. You have to continue to use the momentum you have built as you have gone through this book.

Get Ready for Growth

You are now ready to move forward with this book and start the journal entries that can help you meet your shadow self and make peace with the shadowy parts of your personality.

SHADOW WORK JOURNAL EXERCISES

"Never fear shadows. They simply mean there's a light shining somewhere nearby."

– Unknown -

THE JOURNEY OF THE SHADOW WORK

In this journal, you will find a series of exercises that will guide you in discovering your inner shadow and help you overcome your personal limits. However, to achieve these results, you will need to commit constantly and dedicate time every day to face your fears and insecurities.

You will be able to recognize and manage your emotions, understand your behaviors, and become the best version of yourself. Remember that each exercise will take you deeper, confronting strong emotions and intense sensations, so always be aware of who you are now and why you have chosen to embark on this journey.

Take this path seriously and approach it in the way that you deem most appropriate and correct. Only then can you achieve the results you seek and improve your inner life. Your commitment and dedication will lead to significant changes in your life, just as it has for many others.

Facing Your Fears

No matter how strong or resilient you are, you cannot escape fear. Fear is a vital part of human nature because it is an alert that something might be wrong, and it prepares your body to respond promptly to potential dangers that may arise. No, it's not fun, but your fear is something engrained in you to promote survival. It is something you need to survive.

Much of the shadow self is fear, and your fears can be so deeply buried that you lose track of their root. It is by facing your fears that you can overcome them and become more resilient in the face of challenges. Listening to your fear is a fantastic tool, but you cannot let it run your life. If you do, you make your life smaller when you could be making it bigger.

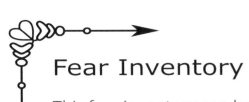
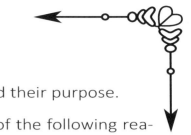

Fear Inventory

This fear inventory can help you identify them and their purpose.

I am afraid of _____ because of the following reasons:

_____

_____

_____

This fear causes me to _____

_____, _____, and _____

_____. I know this fear has a

purpose, but I want to _____

even though I'm scared. When I finally face all the fears I have, I want

to _____

_____

_____

Fear Memory

Describe a moment when you felt a lot of fear. Tell your story however you see fit.

_____

_____

_____

_____

_____

_____

_____

_____

_____

_____

_____

_____

_____

_____

_____

_____

_____

Showing Your Shadow Self Kindness

It's easy to make your shadow self the enemy, to suggest that the shadow is the heart of all your problems or that it is a monster taking up residence in your body; however, those kinds of statements don't capture the nuance of the shadow self. Your shadow self can cause you a lot of problems, but that doesn't mean it is evil. It is part of you, just like your arms or legs are part of you. When you show your shadow self compassion, you create a meaningful connection to those parts of you, which is essential in shadow work.

How I Treat My Shadow Self

Now that you have done some work understanding your shadow self, think about the ways you have treated yourself. Have you been cruel? Have you been neglectful? How would you like to change your behavior going forward to be kinder to your shadow self?

_____

_____

_____

_____

_____

_____

_____

_____

_____

_____

_____

_____

_____

_____

_____

_____

_____

_____

Dealing With Trauma

The traumatized brain acts differently, and it can become fixated on the trauma rather than the present. It comes in many forms, but no matter the type of trauma you have, it likely has a big impact on your life, even if you aren't initially aware of how much it may influence you. Today, you will learn to unpack your trauma and start to understand the major life events that your shadow self may try to suppress to protect you from negative feelings.

Even if you don't think of yourself as having trauma, you should reflect on the biggest obstacles you have endured in your life, which every person experiences to some extent. Furthermore, many people minimalize their experiences, but to deal with them, you have to confront and begin to process all the things that have made your life tumble off balance and have shaped your view of the world.

Trauma in Your Body

How does your trauma make your body feel? Think about the physical sensations that the hardest parts of your life have on you and the way your body remembers what you have been through.

_____

_____

_____

_____

_____

_____

_____

_____

_____

_____

_____

_____

_____

_____

_____

_____

_____

Finding Courage

Too many people think that courage is about not being afraid; however, courage is so much more than that, and you need to be afraid to have courage. Courage is all about being afraid and doing the things that make you happy anyway. It is about acknowledging the pain and worry of your shadow self while also recognizing that you cannot let those negative feelings stop you. Doing anything worthwhile means taking risks, and you've got to find the courage to take those risks.

I Have Courage

Think about a time when you were scared but chose to face your fears anyway. How did you feel? What made you so scared in the first place? What good outcomes came from pushing through your fears?

_____

_____

_____

_____

_____

_____

_____

_____

_____

_____

_____

_____

_____

_____

_____

_____

_____

_____

_____

Tug of War Within You

Internal conflicts are the number one thing to lead to indecision. When you don't know what to do in a situation, it's often because you are battling two parts of yourself. Often, your shadow self is the stronger force and may lead to you making decisions that protect the things you are ashamed of rather than boosting the things that make you proud.

Internal War

Imagine that there's a war happening within your brain. What does this war look like? Who are the parties involved? What are the stakes? Use these questions to shape your response, but feel free to imagine beyond these questions.

_____

_____

_____

_____

_____

_____

_____

_____

_____

_____

_____

_____

_____

_____

_____

_____

_____

_____

What Have You Lost?

Loss is a painful and unavoidable part of life. There's no reason to linger on all the losses and become bitter over them, but it's helpful to acknowledge what you have lost and how those things have influenced your life.

My Grief

Talk about one of the losses that stick with you the most. Consider how this loss has changed you and think about the way the thing or person you lost still positively influences your life.

_____

_____

_____

_____

_____

_____

_____

_____

_____

_____

_____

_____

_____

_____

_____

_____

_____

What Have You Gained?

Think about all the things you have gained in life. These things can be anything that you didn't have before but have now. Thinking of these things can help show you that by focusing on what you have gained, you can stay positive.

Think about something good or exciting that has happened within the past year.

_____

_____

_____

_____

_____

_____

_____

_____

_____

_____

_____

_____

_____

_____

_____

_____

_____

Boundaries and the Shadow Self

Setting boundaries with the people in your life helps you create protective walls around yourself and gives you a safe space to explore your shadow self. You don't want to create too many boundaries that keep everyone out of your life entirely, but you do want to have physical and emotional boundaries in your relationships that specify where another person ends and you begin.

My Boundaries

Discuss some of the boundaries you'd like to put in place in one of your primary relationships. You can also discuss how blurred boundaries have caused issues in the past.

_____

_____

_____

_____

_____

_____

_____

_____

_____

_____

_____

_____

_____

_____

_____

_____

_____

_____

_____

_____

_____

Building Confidence

Confidence is one of the most important elements of life. To feel good about who we are and what we are doing, we need to build more confidence. This confidence gives us a good foundation for everything else in our lives.

People See My Worth

Discuss the qualities that people most compliment you on, or if you struggle to think of something, talk about the good qualities you use the most to get tasks done.

_____

_____

_____

_____

_____

_____

_____

_____

_____

_____

_____

_____

_____

_____

_____

_____

_____

_____

_____

Creating Light

With all this shadow talk, the world can feel like a dark place, but that doesn't have to be the case. In fact, shadow work is all about finding the light. It's about working through the darkness so that you can see the dark parts of you that cannot destroy the light parts of you. The more you confront your shadow, the more you can create the kind of light that gives you fulfillment and joy. There are bright parts of yourself, no matter how dark the place you are in. Hold onto those parts and nurture them.

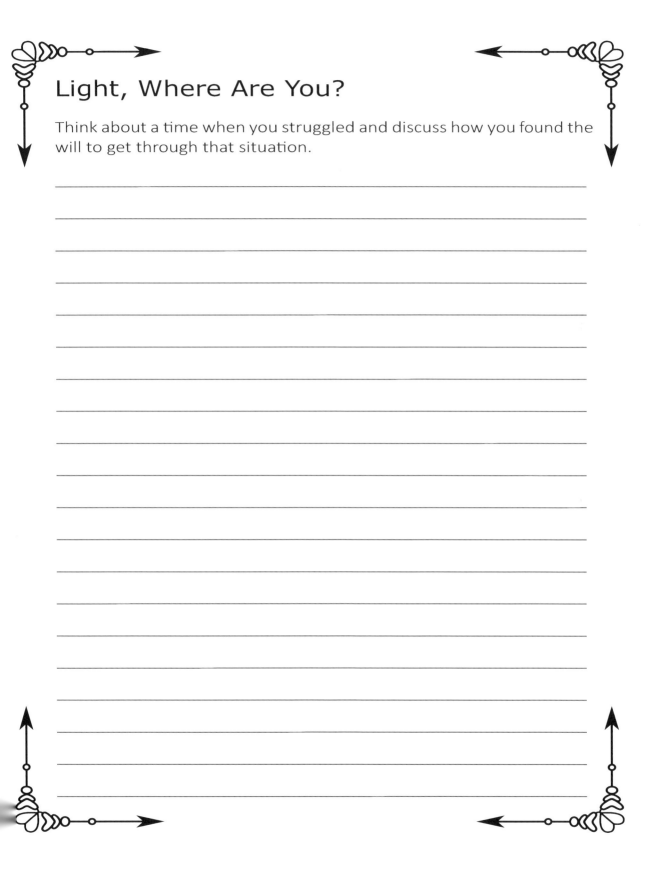

Light, Where Are You?

Think about a time when you struggled and discuss how you found the will to get through that situation.

_____

_____

_____

_____

_____

_____

_____

_____

_____

_____

_____

_____

_____

_____

_____

_____

_____

_____

_____

_____

_____

A Letter to Little You

Your past self has been through a lot, and some of what they have been through could be things that you have inflicted on yourself. Getting in touch with the little version of yourself is an important part of your shadow work because this process emphasizes acknowledging what has happened in your past and the way we all have an inner child within us that represents all the past hurts, hopes, and everything else that we have repressed and shoved into the shadow.

Hello Little Me

Write a letter to your inner child.

_____

_____

_____

_____

_____

_____

_____

_____

_____

_____

_____

_____

_____

_____

_____

_____

_____

_____

_____

_____

_____

The Wonder of Flaws

People were not built to be perfect. We all have limitations and make mistakes. These mistakes are things that often result in us feeling ashamed. Fortunately, mistakes don't have to be so devastating. Shadow work helps us confront our flaws and leads us to have more understanding of how we can use our flaws to do better going forward.

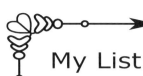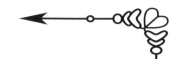

My List of Flaws

Write ten of your flaws.

1. _____
2. _____
3. _____
4. _____
5. _____
6. _____
7. _____
8. _____
9. _____
10. _____

My Worst Flaw

Take some time to reflect on the flaw you hate the most about yourself.

_____

_____

_____

_____

_____

_____

_____

_____

_____

_____

_____

_____

_____

_____

_____

_____

_____

Truth or Shadow

The shadow self often obscures the truth, and the cognitive distortions created by the shadow self are often lies you tell yourself based on faulty associations. For example, a person who gets sick after eating grapes may become afraid of eating all grapes, even if the sickness wasn't actually caused by the grapes and was just a stomach bug. The brain makes connections all the time, and it can make connections where they don't factually exist. Thus, we must learn to distinguish truth from shadow.

The Lies You Tell Yourself

Discuss a lie that you have told yourself and unpack how that lie is related to something you don't like about yourself or dark parts of you.

_____

_____

_____

_____

_____

_____

_____

_____

_____

_____

_____

_____

_____

_____

_____

_____

_____

_____

_____

_____

_____

_____

Making Mantras

Mantras are statements you use to encourage yourself and redirect yourself when you are struggling. They are usually short so that you can repeat them often. An example of a mantra is, "I can get through this with the strength of my character." You can make a mantra for anything and use it in any situation.

My Mantras

Write five mantras. They can be related to whatever areas of your life you want. Feel free to write extras as well.

1. _____

_____

_____

_____

2. _____

_____

_____

_____

3. _____

_____

_____

_____

4. _____

_____

_____

_____

5. _____

_____

_____

_____

Mirror, Mirror on the Wall

If you have a bad relationship with your shadow self, it's common to have a distorted sense of self-image. This self-image can refer to how you see yourself physically and how you see yourself internally. In any case, disconnection from the shadow can increase your self-doubts, and you can start to see everything you are in a negative light. You start to feel like something is wrong with you, and your eyes can even fool you when you look in the mirror. It's time to take back your self-image and find the good qualities in your reflection.

What Do I See?

Stand in front of the mirror and write about what you see. Once you have dealt with your physical self, go deeper and try to determine what you "see" within yourself. Try to look into your eyes without looking away and try to understand what you feel.

Are you afraid? Look away? Do you know the person you are looking at in the mirror?

_____

_____

_____

_____

_____

_____

_____

_____

_____

_____

_____

_____

_____

_____

_____

_____

_____

_____

Finding Balance

Life is full of extremes. These extremes can cause you to overreact or underreact to certain stimuli. For example, when some people are depressed, they may lose their appetite, while other people may eat mindlessly and become extra hungry. Both behaviors can be harmful, and it is by finding a balance that people find the healthiest. The unaddressed shadow self-pushes us towards extremes because it makes it hard to think clearly. For instance, if you've had many bad romantic relationships, the shadow self may subconsciously urge you to avoid relationships to avoid future hurt. This avoidance can lead to loneliness. In this situation, a lack of balance prevents you from living happily. It is by acknowledging that relationships can hurt you, but they are worthy, calculated risks that you can feel harmonious.

Balance Beam

Imagine you are on a balance beam. There are two distinct areas on either side of you. What do these areas look like? And what can you do to remain balanced between them without falling to any one side?

_____

_____

_____

_____

_____

_____

_____

_____

_____

_____

_____

_____

_____

_____

_____

_____

_____

_____

_____

Bad Decisions

Think of decisions you regret. Why did you make those decisions? What have you learned that would help you make better decisions?

_____

_____

_____

_____

_____

_____

_____

_____

_____

_____

_____

_____

_____

_____

_____

_____

_____

_____

_____

_____

_____

_____

_____

Shadowy Habits

Habits shape much of what you do each day. Think about your morning routine: that is a habit. A habit is like a shortcut that enables you to easily complete tasks you have done before without putting in so much mental effort. Habits are useful because they allow you to save your energy for other tasks, but not all habits are good for you. Some are driven by the subconscious hurting of the shadow. For example, someone who abuses substances may try to turn off their shadow self through numbing behaviors associated with certain substances. This habit seems appealing on some level because it gives emotional release, but in the long run, it is harmful. Awareness of shadow-driven habits can help you replace those bad habits with healthier ones.

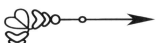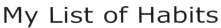

My List of Habits

Write ten of your habits.

1. _____

2. _____

3. _____

4. _____

5. _____

6. _____

7. _____

8. _____

9. _____

10. _____

My Worst Habit

Think about your worst habit and the impact it has on your life. What habits could you choose to do instead of your worst habits?

_____

_____

_____

_____

_____

_____

_____

_____

_____

_____

_____

_____

_____

_____

_____

_____

_____

_____

_____

_____

_____

_____

_____

_____

_____

The Shadow and Stress

The shadow self takes any negative stress you have and magnifies it with the stress of the past. When you get stuck in your head, and the stress is building up, it signals that you have some level of disconnect with your own internal world. By taking some time to process what is happening within, you can overcome some of your negative stress.

Today I Was Stressed

Write about a time today or in the past week when stress has negatively impacted you. What events surrounded that stress, and how did you try to deal with what you were feeling?

_____
_____
_____
_____
_____
_____
_____
_____
_____
_____
_____
_____
_____
_____
_____
_____
_____
_____
_____
_____
_____
_____
_____

The Anxious Caveman

Your caveman's brain is wired to keep you safe. This inner caveman acts quickly when it feels like it is in danger because when humans were still cavemen, we had to do so to survive. When something bad happens to you, your caveman's brain remembers, and it tries to avoid situations that resemble the bad things that happened. Additionally, your brain feels panicked when it senses danger, even when there is no real danger. A person who is scared of spiders because they saw a news report of increased deadly spider bites may logically know that the spider isn't likely to hurt them, but that doesn't mean they won't be anxious around that spider.

Fight, Flight, Or Freeze

Think about when your caveman instincts last took over, and you felt the urge to fight, flee, or freeze. What caused that response? How did you react? What did you feel after?

_____

_____

_____

_____

_____

_____

_____

_____

_____

_____

_____

_____

_____

_____

_____

_____

_____

_____

_____

Accepting Compassion

For many people with a lot of shadow work to do, accepting compassion from other people can be a challenge, but learning to accept the kindness of others helps you be more forthcoming and reduces shame and self-doubt.

Being Cruel

Think of times you've treated yourself with cruelty. Consider whether you would have treated your best friend or a little version of yourself that same way. Why did you think it was okay to do so toward yourself? How could you show yourself more compassion?

_____

_____

_____

_____

_____

_____

_____

_____

_____

_____

_____

_____

_____

_____

_____

_____

_____

_____

_____

_____

Affirm Your Future

Affirmations mean that you make phrases about what you want to happen as if they have already happened. For example, if you want to be wealthy, you could say, "I am wealthy," or if you want romantic relationships, you could say, "I am falling in love." These types of statements prime your brain to create the outcomes you are wishing for.

Affirmation of Dreams

Write about the future you want in the present tense, as if you already have it. Imagine experiencing it vividly right now. If you struggle to get started, use some "I am" statements.

_____

_____

_____

_____

_____

_____

_____

_____

_____

_____

_____

_____

_____

_____

_____

_____

_____

_____

_____

_____

_____

_____

_____

Your Own Obituary

It may seem dark but writing your own obituary can be a useful tool for defining what you want your life to be. It helps you think not just about your future, but of your legacy. Your life goes on in certain ways after you have died, so you cannot just think about the life you will live, but you also want to think about the impressions you will leave. These kinds of thoughts can be scary if you aren't used to dealing with them, but as you get more in touch with the potential of death and the fleeting nature of life, you will start to emerge from your fears and embrace the precious moments you have.

My Obituary

Write an obituary about yourself, detailing how you would like to be remembered after you have died.

_____

_____

_____

_____

_____

_____

_____

_____

_____

_____

_____

_____

_____

_____

_____

_____

_____

_____

_____

_____

_____

_____

Trying New Things

When you try new things, you challenge the expectations you have about yourself and the world. When you do the same things over and over, you get bored, and you don't challenge yourself to be better. You don't have to reinvent the wheel to try new things. Trying new things can come in small steps, like trying a new recipe or driving a new route to work.

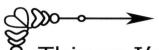
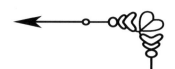

Things I'd Like to Try

Write about fifteen things you'd like to try. Choose one of those things to try today.

1. _____
2. _____
3. _____
4. _____
5. _____
6. _____
7. _____
8. _____
9. _____
10. _____
11. _____
12. _____
13. _____
14. _____
15. _____

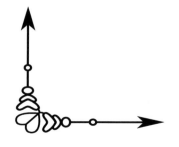
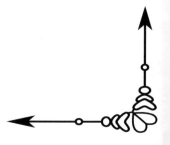

Meditation Minutes

Meditation is a useful technique that challenges you to sit in a peaceful place for several minutes. During this time, you focus on the sensations in your body and imagine energy flowing through you. For example, you can imagine that there is light spreading through your body. This light goes in through your head, and it exits your extremities. When you can think in this way, you begin to feel calm. This calmness follows you into moments of stress, allowing you to be more resilient.

Try your first meditation without trying too hard, take it as a new experience to understand your thoughts.

Post Mediation Reflection

After meditating, take some time to reflect on your experience.

Before meditation I felt:

_____

_____

_____

_____

_____

During meditation I felt:

_____

_____

_____

_____

_____

After meditation I felt:

_____

_____

_____

_____

_____

What thoughts reoccurred during meditation:

_____

_____

_____

_____

_____

What did I observe during meditation:

_____

_____

_____

_____

_____

Other thoughts related to meditation:

_____

_____

_____

_____

_____

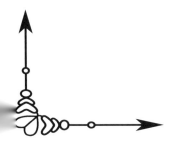

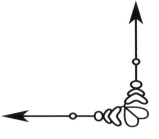

Finding Hope in the Dark

Remember that when you are in a dark place, there is always hope. It may seem that there is no chance of things getting better, but when you feel that way, it is essential that you remember that there's always hope in the darkness and holding onto that hope can lead you to the light. Your shadow self doesn't want to consume you with its darkness; it wants to show you the brightness of life through awareness and contrast.

My Darkest Hour

At what moment of your life did you feel the least amount of hope?
What did you do to pull through your darkest hour?

What are the feelings you felt before and what did you feel afterward?

_____

_____

_____

_____

_____

_____

_____

_____

_____

_____

_____

_____

_____

_____

_____

_____

_____

_____

_____

_____

_____

_____

_____

Rewriting Your Thoughts

Your nasty thoughts may convince you that you can't d or you shouldn't do certain things. These thoughts are often built upon faulty foundations, which is why you need to address them and start to rewrite any thought that is keeping you from being your genuine self.

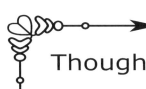
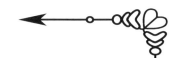

Thought Transformation

In this exercise, you will learn to take a negative thought and make it into a positive one.

Example:

Scenario: You are stuck as you work on a project. You don't know what to do next.

Negative Thought: "I am stupid."

Thought Transformation: "I am unaware of the best practices to use for this project, but I have the skills required to do some additional research and ask for extra help when needed."

Now, you can try it for yourself!

Scenario:

_____

_____

_____

Negative Thought:

_____

_____

_____

Thought Transformation:

_____

_____

_____

Negative thoughts list

Write about ten negative thoughts that you would like to change. After you have chosen them repeat the exercise.

1. _____

2. _____

3. _____

4. _____

5. _____

6. _____

7. _____

8. _____

9. _____

10. _____

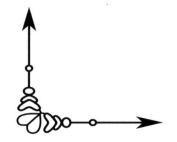
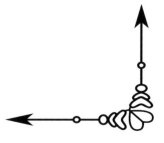

Defining a Higher Power

Every person needs to have a higher power. This higher power commonly comes in the form of a deity like God; however, a higher power is more than just religious. Your higher power is whatever thing greater than yourself that shapes your life. Your higher power can be something like nature or another concept like love. Finding this higher power is so important in shadow work because when you're dealing with your shadow, you want to be honest with yourself about who you are and all the elements that shape your perspective of the world.

Defining Your Higher Power

My higher power is _____, and I acknowledge this
power by _____

_____

_____

_____

I hold this higher power because I believe that

_____

_____

_____

_____

I want to engage more with my higher power by

_____

_____

_____

_____

My higher power makes my life fuller because

_____

_____

_____

_____

Dear Higher Power

Write a letter of appreciation to your higher power.

_____

_____

_____

_____

_____

_____

_____

_____

_____

_____

_____

_____

_____

_____

_____

_____

_____

_____

_____

_____

_____

_____

_____

_____

The Magic in Yourself

You are magic. You're not magic in the common definition of the word, but you are magic in that you can create your reality. There are many things that you cannot change in life, but when you learn to focus on what you can do, you start to find magic in yourself. You enable yourself to adapt to life's changes, and you empower yourself to bring to life all the dreams you want to come true. Your mind is more powerful than you know, and by working with your brain rather than against it, you can discover the magic in yourself.

The Magic in Me

Imagine that you have all the magic you could ever want, and you can use this magic to do anything. How would you use your magic? Also, think about what makes you feel the most powerful.

_____

_____

_____

_____

_____

_____

_____

_____

_____

_____

_____

_____

_____

_____

_____

_____

_____

_____

_____

_____

_____

_____

_____

_____

"The best political, social, and spiritual work we can do is to withdraw the projection of our shadow onto others."

– Carl Jung -

CONCLUSION

FINAL REFLECTIONS

It's hard to believe, but you have reached to end of this book. You have done an outstanding of transformative action, and that's something you should be so proud of. In transformation journeys, many people give up after the first couple of weeks, unable or unwilling to put in the time and energy to do the hard but necessary work for self-growth. You have made it through all the way, and I want you to celebrate this successful victory. However, you also must acknowledge that the end of this book doesn't mean it is the end of your shadow work journey. Before you go, I want you to consider where you started, where you are now, and what you can do to ensure you have prolonged progress.

What You Have Learned

The lessons in this book are many to absorb, but by working consistently they are much more digestible. That doesn't mean you won't still feel overwhelmed. As you finish the prompts, you may be feeling nervous or not sure what to do with yourself. With that in mind, it helps to organize your thoughts and gain perspective on some of the key points that you have learned, points that you can carry on throughout your life.

You have learned many techniques in this book to help you be more in touch with your shadow self. These techniques have shown you that your shadow self exists. You may not have known that you had a shadow self before, let alone how to use it in your best interests.

Shadow work is a powerful tool defined by Carl Jung, but the sense of having a "dark side" beneath the surface has long been known and sensed by humans. This dark side does not contain just darkness because when you hide certain dark parts of yourself, you also have to hide certain light parts. The shadow is often shaped by trauma, pain, and negativity, but by illuminating the hard-to-reconcile parts of yourself, you free your brain to work more productively.

This book has challenged you to learn more about yourself through analysis and self-reflection. You have been urged to look at yourself in new ways. This task is the hardest that any person can do because it forces you to ask yourself if how you define yourself matches who you really are. Shadow work is terrifying in that way, but it allows you to realign your genuine self with the person you present to the world. When you feel aligned, you feel at peace with who you are and the decisions you are making.

More than just yourself, you have learned the power of shadow work for the relationships and activities you have beyond yourself. The world is yours for the taking, and the opportunities of what you can do are only limited by the barriers you place around yourself. The more you isolate yourself from the chance you could take, the smaller your world becomes. Having such a small world can make you feel desperate for more but make you too afraid to reach for more. Often, the feelings that shape those fears are within the shadow self, so by acknowledging the shadow, you can face the things that hold you back and prevent you from being a more engaged part of this world.

Journaling has been a fundamental part of your experience, and it's something that has shown you how to reflect upon yourself and your tendencies. It has helped you define what you want, what motivates you, and your role in the world beyond yourself as an individual. Journaling is partly introspection, creativity, and mindfulness. It combines a lot of positive features to create more influence. You don't need to spend a lot of time each day journaling. In fact, even just fifteen minutes can make you feel a lot better during shadow work. The main goal is to create a consistent schedule because your shadow self will respond to consistent engagement.

All the lessons you have learned come together to create a powerful medicine for feeling disconnected, fearful, or unsure of the path you want to take. You don't have all the answers to life and what it means from this book, but you have found the answers to give your own life meaning and find your purpose. You have the fuel you need to get excited about the future rather than dread it. Your shadow self may seem like darkness, but in the light, you can see that it is so much more. It is that part of you that you try to hide, but it also holds a part of you that wants so desperately to thrive.

Mental Wellness Check

Very good! You have concluded your journey to discover your shadow. You are now closer to being a freer version of yourself, no longer hindered by your shadow self. Because this process takes so much emotional work, it's important to check how you're doing mentally. Think about how you feel about this process and which emotions have been more dominant.

If you're struggling mentally, consider whether you might need more mental help to support you through this journey. If you've unearthed memories or feelings that are too difficult to handle, a professional can help you get checked in and address your specific issues.

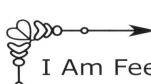

I Am Feeling...

Circle some of the things that you have been feeling.

Angry	Anxious
Happy	Stressed
Generous	Disconnected
Sad	Lonely
Hurt	Apathetic
Friendly	Joyous
Upset	Satisfied
Smart	Reflective
Isolated	Mean
Rude	Funny
Unburdened	Distressed
Ruminative	Light
Unsure	Confused
Scared	Insatiable
Upbeat	Competent
Irritable	Social
Beautiful	

Reflecting on the Experience

Write about how your mental health has been influenced by the process so far.

_____

_____

_____

_____

_____

_____

_____

_____

_____

_____

_____

_____

_____

_____

_____

_____

_____

_____

_____

_____

_____

_____

_____

_____

The Shadow Still Exists

There's no escaping your shadow. No matter how much shadow work you do, your shadow is still going to exist. Therefore, you can't just address and then forget your shadow self. You have to put in the work to continue to be in harmony with your shadow self. This process can seem daunting, but you have learned all the skills you need to continue with your work and create a sustainable mindset.

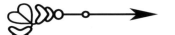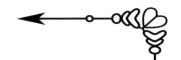

Here We Go Shadow

Draw a picture of your shadow again. Don't think too much about what your shadow looks like. Draw this portrait based on your instinctive and imaginative idea of what your shadow looks like. Even your shadow doesn't have to be human!

Go back to review the shadow you drew at the beginning of the path. Try to compare them and tell me what you understand about your shadow.

_____

_____

_____

_____

_____

_____

_____

_____

_____

_____

_____

_____

_____

_____

_____

_____

_____

_____

_____

_____

_____

_____

_____

Gratitude Refresh

You have learned the power of gratitude, but gratitude is a process that requires you to check in often. It's been many days since you've done gratitude work, which is why it's so important that you reorient yourself and make sure that you are still taking gratitude seriously. Think about the things you were grateful for when you last journaled about gratitude. Do those things still apply at this moment? How has your gratitude evolved? How well have you done at continuing to be grateful in your daily life?

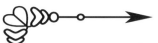

Gratitude List

Write fifteen things that you are grateful for. These things can be as small or as big as you'd like them to be.

1. _____
2. _____
3. _____
4. _____
5. _____
6. _____
7. _____
8. _____
9. _____
10. _____
11. _____
12. _____
13. _____
14. _____
15. _____

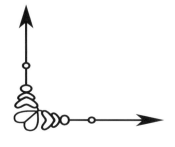
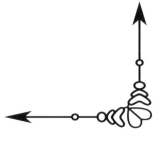

Progress Check Out

This is the final check-in of this book! Congratulations on making it this far and for putting in the hard work required to be consistent with your journaling practice. It hasn't been easy, but you have powered through the hard work that you have been asked to do.

- *How was this journey?*
- *Have you had moments of reflection?*
- *Have you spent moments working on yourself?*
- *Have you worked on your fears, your anxieties, your traumas, and your memories?*
- *Do you understand what is really important to you?*
- *Who are the most important people to you?*
- *Do you have ideas about what makes you happy and what gives you well-being?*

Tell what you felt with this journal, this is the last exercise of your journal, enjoy it!

_____

_____

_____

_____

_____

_____

_____

_____

_____

_____

_____

Ten Things I've Learned

Write ten things you've learned so far on this journey.

1. _____

2. _____

3. _____

4. _____

5. _____

6. _____

7. _____

8. _____

9. _____

10._____

WHAT'S NEXT

There's a lot that you can still do to take on your shadow self. If you still have a sense of disconnect or feel like your shadow work is incomplete, that's completely normal. It's hard to make a change in a short time, especially if you are dealing with deeply ingrained things. Major feelings and deeply entrenched habits within the shadow self are ongoing battles, but the more you practice healthy handling of your shadow self, the more the practice becomes second nature.

Maintaining Your Progress

Maintenance is one of the most important steps of continued shadow work. Fortunately, this process is a lot easier because you have already established many of the necessary habits, and it shouldn't feel too much harder to use maintenance habits. Maintenance is all about staying in touch with your shadow work and being more mindful of your unconscious behaviors. When something doesn't feel right, instead of pushing it down, you can learn to ask questions and see what is really going on.

To maintain your progress, you should continue to keep a journal. You have enough experience with journaling that you should be able to self-direct yourself in the process, but if you struggle, using prompts can get you going. It can also be useful to do "free writes" when you free write, you write about whatever comes to mind and let your writing flow. You can also start to incorporate journaling alternatives. For example, you can keep voice notes reflecting on your experiences, draw what's happening, or combine several other means to make your journaling more dynamic.

Any time you think you may be going off track, don't give up your shadow work altogether; instead, work to get back on track. Many people quit when they feel they have messed up, but maintenance is all about learning that you will never do things perfectly, and your best bet is remembering that mistakes are there for you to learn how to do better going forward.

A Long Relationship With Your Shadow

The goal is to avoid closing this book and going back to how things were, which means that you have to make long-standing relationships with your shadow. Whether you put the work in or not, you have a relationship with your shadow. You get to define what the nature of that relationship looks like, just as you shape all other relationships in your life. Thus, you could go back to your old ways, or you can choose to evolve in ways that better reflect the life you want to live and the things that give you joy.

You Can Always Go Back

You always have the option to go back through the journal entries in this book and cycle through them again. When you are struggling to keep up certain practices independently, the prompts you have already completed can be used again to get you back on track. The exciting thing about these prompts is that because people are so dynamic, whatever you deem right will change dramatically as you go through life; therefore, the answers you have each time you use the prompts will be new and reflect different elements of your life. Your answers highlight where you are and what you want when you write them.

Sharing the Growth

It's a great idea to share this journey with other people who you think can use it. At the beginning of this book, you may have thought that you were the only one to experience the things that you were experiencing. That couldn't be further from the truth, and the truth is that people all around the world are struggling with their shadow selves. They are going through their lives feeling like something isn't right, unable to be their fullest selves, but they don't know how to make the change that will enable them to have the life they want.

Many people in your life may be struggling with their shadow selves without even realizing it; as a result, by making them conscious of shadow work, you can give them the gift of confronting the dark parts of their lives and learning to work through them safely and healthily. No one should have to suffer alone or in silence. Life is hard enough without good relationships, and shadow work never has to be done in isolation. You can spread the useful information in this book and show this resource to other people. This book makes a great gift that will keep on giving.

Shadow work is a connective experience for many people. When you share the things you want to hide, it brightens your life because secrets that are freed from your shadow are no longer burdens that you have to carry alone. It's incredibly liberating to grow through shadow work, so shadow work is a great gift to give people in your life who are struggling. Even people who don't have any major troubles or hardships can benefit from shadow work because we all have struggles, and we all have shadows selves. While our shadows can seem scary, they are always valuable because they are part of ourselves, and that's remarkable.

Wrap Up

The time and energy you have put into this book are greatly appreciated. Hopefully, you have found some of the internal peace you are looking for, and you have begun to push yourself to think in new ways. It is still early in your shadow work journey, and this book highlights how much growth can be found through consistent journaling and shadow work. Thanks so much for reading, and if you found this book useful, a review would be appreciated. Good luck with your journey. You're fully capable of continuing this powerful work.

Congratulations!

You have finished your journey!

If you're fully enjoying this journal, it's always appreciated if you leave a review of my Journal.

This would help to share and find this knowledge more easily for people who are looking for it!

FREE SPACES

FREE SPACES

Your support is important to me!

Great things can start from a small gesture!

Leave a sincere review to support my work.

This would help to share and find this knowledge more easily to people who are looking for it.

References Quotes

C. G. JUNG, C.W. Vol 16: Practice of Psychotherapy, "the thing a person has no wish to be."

ST. CATHERINE OF SIENA, "It is only through shadows that one comes to know the light."

C. G. JUNG, C.W. Vol 9 (Part 1): Archetypes and the Collective Unconscious, Carl Jung says the shadow self "displays a number of good qualities, such as normal instincts, appropriate reactions, realistic insights, creative impulses, etc.".

The Collected Works of C.G. Jung: Psychology and alchemy (ed. 1953), "There is no light without shadow and no psychic wholeness without imperfection."

C. G. JUNG, "Alchemical Studies, Vol 13", "One does not become enlightened by imagining figures of light, but by making the darkness conscious."

CONNIE ZWEIG, "Shadow-making happens in families and makes us who we are. It leads to shadow-work, which makes us who we can become."

UNKNOWN, "Never fear shadows. They simply mean there's a light shining somewhere nearby."

C. G. JUNG, "The best political, social, and spiritual work we can do is to withdraw the projection of our shadow onto others."

REFERENCES QUOTES

Jung, C. G. " 'Modern Man in Search of a Soul', Ch. 11 pg 234-235, "We cannot change anything unless we accept it".

Jung, C. G. "knowing your own darkness is the best method for dealing with the darkness of other people. It's the confidence and self-assurance within ourselves that allows us to have the strength to deal with everyday life. While it's true the journey

Jung, C. G. "There's no coming to consciousness without pain.".

Jung, C. G. "I am not what happened to me; I am what I choose to become.".

Jung, C. G. "the most terrifying thing is to accept oneself completely.".

Jung, C. G. "There's no coming to conscious without pain."

Jung, C. G. "To confront a person with his shadow is to show him his own light."

REFERENCES

Erika Stoerkel. "The Science and Research on Gratitude and Happiness." PositivePsychology.com, June 23, 2022. https://positivepsychology.com/gratitude-happiness-research/#science-and-research.

John M. Grohol, Psy.D. "The Connection between Mental & Physical Health." Psych Central. Psych Central, February 25, 2009. https://psychcentral.com/blog/the-connection-between-mental-physical-health#1.

Kluger, Jeffrey. "Consciousness: It's Less than You Think." Time. Time, June 26, 2015. https://time.com/3937351/consciousness-unconsciousness-brain/.

"Mental Health Disorder Statistics." Johns Hopkins Medicine, November 19, 2019. https://www.hopkinsmedicine.org/health/wellness-and-prevention/mental-health-disorder-statistics.

Nattrauma. "Trauma Statistics & Facts." Coalition for National Trauma Research, December 21, 2021. https://www.nattrauma.org/trauma-statistics-facts/.

Othon, Jack E. "Carl Jung and the Shadow: The Ultimate Guide to the Human Dark Side." HighExistence, August 7, 2020. https://highexistence.com/carl-jung-shadow-guide-unconscious/.

"The Power of Positive Thinking." Johns Hopkins Medicine, November 1, 2021. https://www.hopkinsmedicine.org/health/wellness-and-prevention/the-power-of-positive-thinking.

"The Shadow." Society of Analytical Psychology, May 13, 2022. https://www.thesap.org.uk/articles-on-jungian-psychology-2/about-analysis-and-therapy/the-shadow/.

"A Showcase for the Mind-Body Connection." Monitor on Psychology. Ame-

rican Psychological Association. Accessed August 2, 2022. https://www.
apa.org/monitor/sep05/showcase.

"Statistics for Mental Trauma: How Common Is IT & Who It Affects." FHE
Health – Addiction & Mental Health Care. Accessed August 2, 2022. https://fherehab.com/trauma/statistics.

"What Is Gratitude? 5 Ways to Practice Being Thankful." What Is Gratitude?
5 Ways to Practice Being Thankful, April 30, 2021. https://www.betterup.
com/blog/gratitude-definition-how-to-practice.

Made in United States
Troutdale, OR
10/19/2023

13443720R00128